Annette Lyster

Riding out the Gale

Vol. III

Annette Lyster

Riding out the Gale
Vol. III

ISBN/EAN: 9783337051587

Printed in Europe, USA, Canada, Australia, Japan

Cover: Foto ©ninafisch / pixelio.de

More available books at **www.hansebooks.com**

A Novel.

BY
ANNETTE LYSTER.

IN THREE VOLUMES.
VOL. III.

London:
SAMUEL TINSLEY,
10, SOUTHAMPTON STREET, STRAND.
1877.
(*All Rights Reserved.*)

CHAPTER I.

AT about one o'clock next day, Dr. Mostyn arrived at the Abbey, and asked to see Sir Lionel. After a moment's delay, he was asked to go to the library, whither he was accompanied by Haidee, who had joined him in the gallery. Sir Lionel frowned ominously when he saw her.

"Good-morning, Dr. Mostyn. You wish to speak to me, I believe? Oblige me by deferring your remarks for a short period. Haidee, I shall be busy for a time—favour me by withdrawing."

"I cannot, papa," Haidee said gently. "Nor need I. For I saw Singleton yesterday, and was aware that this visit was intended."

"You saw Singleton! Dr. Mostyn, how did this occur? You had my express commands that my son should not see any one, unless sent by me."

"I did not think that those orders extended to his sister, Sir Lionel."

Sir Lionel's face was dark with anger and dismay. Never very bright, he was utterly helpless when taken by surprise; and in his perplexity he wished for the aid of his trusty John. He rang the bell, exclaiming, "I must see John—this is very extraordinary—very unforeseen. Haidee, how did you become aware —I had intended to spare you the knowledge of—oh—Pierce, send Mr. John here."

"Mr. John is out, Sir Lionel."

"Send men to look for him, and let them tell him to come here immediately. Haidee, your presence here is unnecessary : you had better withdraw."

"I cannot, Sir Lionel. I am the only friend that Singleton has at hand, and I will not fail him. I think the person whose presence is unnecessary is John : surely you are able to listen to what Dr. Mostyn has to say without his help."

Sir Lionel coloured furiously.

"Undoubtedly I am. Has Dr. Mostyn any communication to make to me concerning the unhappy young man whom I consigned to his care?"

"I have, Sir Lionel. Having carefully considered Mr. Trelawney's case, I am happy to be able to assure you that he is not mad."

"Not mad!" Sir Lionel echoed, with evident surprise. "Is it possible? I had no idea that a cure so rapid was to be looked for."

"But there is no cure in this case, Sir Lionel. Mr. Trelawney never was mad."

"Dr. Mostyn! you forget yourself strangely. I sent my son to your establishment—is it likely that I should have done so unless I was perfectly convinced that he was a fit subject for your care? And surely, I must be the best judge in this matter!"

"With all respect, Sir Lionel, I cannot agree with you there. I suspect that the truth is that you are of a very reserved, self-contained disposition, and that your son is quite the reverse: impulsive, outspoken, frank to a fault, and probably headstrong. But all this, even when carried to excess, does not constitute madness. You have mistaken eccentricity for madness— but your son is perfectly sane, and is no fitting inmate of a lunatic asylum. No honest physician would keep him six months."

"Good heavens, Dr. Mostyn! do you not see—are you blind to the consequences of your decision? If my son is not insane, what is he? You are aware that he attempted my life?"

Haidee was going to speak, but Dr. Mostyn made her a sign to be silent.

"I am aware that he has been accused of it; but he utterly denies it, and declares that he can prove that he was at a considerable distance when the shot was fired. He suspects that the real culprit is a negro servant whom you had recently discharged in disgrace—this idea was put into his head by the fact that the man who was seen by the butler wore a Scotch cap, which he says you may remember the negro always wore."

"A Scotch cap—my servant—I never remarked what he wore. But Singleton certainly wore such a cap on that day. And the rifle was his."

"Yes, he had very carelessly left it leaning against a tree somewhere," Dr. Mostyn answered, again forestalling the impetuous words which were ready on Haidee's lips. "I told him yesterday when we were talking over it after dinner—he dined with me last night—that he almost deserved to get into a scrape for his heedlessness; and he said that this was not the only scrape he had rushed into in the same heedless way. But he declares that if he were at liberty, he would soon free himself from those blots upon his name, which his carelessness and want of judgment have occasioned."

"Impossible! He has deceived you, Dr. Mostyn."

"Well, there is one question on which he cannot have deceived me ; and happily it is the only one with which I am practically concerned. He is not mad, and he cannot remain at Sea View House."

"Then he must go to some other asylum. I must take steps—I must write to—"

"Sir Lionel," said Haidee, "listen to me now. I am to act for Singleton, if you force me to do so ; but I am sure you will not. You have too high a sense of justice not to see that if he is sane, you have no right to immure him in a madhouse, either here or elsewhere."

"Haidee, your interference is most uncalled for—most unseemly ; and you speak in a manner at once impertinent and childish. No right—I surely have every right to protect my own life, and to prevent my son from bringing scandal and disgrace upon my name."

"My dear father, I don't mean to be impertinent, believe me ; but I am only speaking the truth when I say that you have no right, and no power, to keep him in confinement as a lunatic."

"No power! Who is to prevent me?"

"The law will prevent you. I have Singleton's directions to procure legal advice if necessary. That means, if you try to send him to any other asylum; for Dr. Mostyn refuses to keep him."

"I did not understand him to do so," said Sir Lionel uneasily.

"I must refuse, Sir Lionel. I dare not keep him even if I would; it is illegal."

Sir Lionel's colour changed from pale to crimson and back again to a deadly white, and his voice was hoarse and hurried:

"Then I am to let him go loose upon the world, to murder John, or myself, or any one else who may offend him! This cannot be the law! there must surely be some protection to be had!"

"There is," said Dr. Mostyn. "If you accuse him publicly of the attempt upon your life, you will either be convinced of his innocence or protected against his violence. You must either do this, or do as *he* proposes: set him at liberty and give him time to prove his innocence, privately."

Sir Lionel began a furious exclamation, but it died away upon his lips. He rose from his seat, and staggered towards the door; Haidee would have helped him, but he repulsed her roughly and left the room.

"Is your father ill, Miss Trelawney?"

"Oh no! alas—this is no uncommon kind of scene here, Dr. Mostyn. Poor papa! any contradiction excites him so terribly. But can he do any harm, do you think?"

"Do you mean now, at this moment? Oh no, I don't see how he can do that."

Haidee was silent for a few minutes; but Sir Lionel did not return. "I wish he would come back," she said nervously; "I am afraid to go to him, he might be angry—and yet I should like to get him to decide without consulting John, if possible."

"And why should you wish that?" inquired a voice close behind her; and starting round, she found that John had entered by the drawing-room door. He bowed slightly to Dr. Mostyn.

"What is to be decided? and what have I to do with it? Good-morning, Dr. Mostyn. I hope my cousin is well."

"Quite well, Captain Trelawney," replied the doctor; and Haidee added quickly, "And in reply to your other question, John, you *ought* to have nothing to do with this matter. What has startled you? you are pale—you look frightened, I think. What has happened to you?"

"I was frightened, and no wonder! George came running after me to say that Sir Lionel wanted to see me, and that Dr. Mostyn was with him. Naturally I was startled. Where is Sir Lionel?"

"He was here a few minutes ago. I must go and see if he is coming back, if you will excuse me, Dr. Mostyn."

Now I must interrupt myself here to explain that Jasper Phillips, having seen Dr. Mostyn coming to the house, had thought it better to take steps to put John on his guard. Entering the drawing-room softly, he contrived to overhear the few first sentences of the conversation, and had then set off in search of his fellow-conspirator, whom he quickly overtook, in the path to the pond in the oak wood. He had no need to *say* that something of importance had occurred, for John, whose wretched mind was always on the rack, saw it in his face.

"Phillips!" he cried, "all is discovered!"

"No, it is not, nor needn't be, if you will only show the pluck of a field-mouse," Phillips answered rudely.

"But something has happened."

"Of course something has happened; just

what I told you last night *would* happen, if you went on losing time. Now look here, Mr. John Trelawney—George is out looking for you; luckily I knew where you would be, but he'll be here in about ten minutes. In that ten minutes you must make up your mind what you'll do. For if I don't see that you have a decent chance of brazening it out and leaving a hope of doing something in the matter when this blows over, I shall walk back to the house and just tell them all I know."

"You dare not do that! you are too much implicated," John said hurriedly.

"You don't know what I dare. And I can make a good thing of it, even yet. Though I'm sorry enough," he added with a fierce oath, "that I ever had anything to say to you. I thought you a darned sight cleverer than you are; but if you'll behave so as not to lose the game altogether, I'll stand by you still. So—now you know all about it."

" No, I do not," said John angrily, losing his temper suddenly at the man's insolent manner. "You have not told me what has happened yet. I promise you, I wish as sincerely as you can that you had never meddled in the matter; but as you have, you will oblige me by leaving off this blustering nonsense, and tell me plainly what is wrong."

Phillips grew more civil as John grew hot. He answered very meekly:

"Dr. Mostyn is with Sir Lionel. Miss Trelawney met him in the gallery—she expected him. I got into the drawing-room and listened —they are in the library. She knows where the young fellow is, saw him yesterday, and *he* came to say that he isn't mad, and must be let out. Sir Lionel sent for you, and I only dared to wait for a word or two more. Here's George —I hear him coming. I'll hide behind the trees. Send him away, and wait for me."

Phillips disappeared, and George appeared almost at the same moment. It was well for John that the young footman was out of breath and "flustered," as he expressed it himself, or his agitation could hardly have passed unnoticed.

"Sir Lionel wants you, sir—immediate—in the library."

"Yes—very well. I will come at once. You may go."

"Sir Lionel bid me say immediate, sir."

"Very well. You have said it, haven't you? Go now," answered John shortly; and George went on his way, meditating on the vast difference between "the Captain's" manner to servants, and poor Mr. Trelawney's pleasant ways.

"Which I don't believe he ever shot his father —so I don't," was his very illogical conclusion.

"Phillips, he's gone! you can come back. Phillips, it's all up, I think."

"Not if you'll put a bold face on it. Go back to the house as if you knew no more than George told you. Then you're surprised, of course; but if Mostyn says he's not mad, perhaps he isn't. Let him come home to try and prove that it was not him that fired at Sir Lionel. He won't prove that in a hurry; he won't find Black James very easily, and till he finds him he can prove nothing. The one thing you have to mind is, don't let them make a police affair of it; it would most likely all come out then. Just let the lad come home and go looking for James, if he suspects him, as most likely he does. Miss Trelawney will be married in a few weeks, and then we'll see about getting him sent off somewhere. He'll be here alone— who knows what might happen to him?"

They had walked on while Phillips was speaking, and were now at the edge of the wood. Phillips stopped.

"I must go no farther, or they'll see me. You go in through the dining-room and get a peg, and play your game boldly; it's the only game left to you now. If things go wrong we shall have warning, and we'll cut and run; but not empty-handed! Come, Mr. John, you've the brain to do it, if you'll only not show the white feather."

"It's a desperate game! but it's the best we can do. Go you round some other way, Phillips; but go to Sir Lionel's rooms and keep your ears open."

Phillips made his way to the house, and to his master's rooms as quickly as he could. To his great surprise he found Sir Lionel in his sitting-room, looking exceedingly ill. "I'd better see after him," thought Jasper. "He'll go off pop in one of these raging fits one of these fine days; but he must not go off before his precious son. When my gay Captain is the heir he may do as he likes, and the sooner the better."

So he went and stood before his master, the picture of meek deference.

"I fear you are not well, Sir Lionel."

"I am quite well," replied the Baronet, speaking slowly, and with white lips. "I did not ring, Phillips."

"No, Sir Lionel. I was passing by the door, sir. Here is Miss Trelawney, Sir Lionel."

So saying, Jasper the deferential withdrew.

"Papa, are you quite well? You look so pale."

"I am perfectly well, thank you," was the cold reply.

"Will you not come back, then? Dr. Mostyn is waiting for your reply."

"Let him wait. Has John returned?"

"Yes," she said reluctantly, "he is there?"

To her great relief Sir Lionel did not insist upon seeing him in private, but at once walked back, rather slowly and as if with an effort, to the library.

"John, has any one informed you of the object of Dr. Mostyn's visit?"

"No, Sir Lionel; I have but just come in; and he seems unwilling to enlighten me."

"Because I consider that my business is with you alone, Sir Lionel; and experience, which teaches us many a lesson of caution, has taught me that a man's next heir is not always the person to judge of his sanity or insanity."

This Dr. Mostyn said in the most deliberate manner, almost expecting an explosion of wrath from these two tall Trelawneys; but Sir Lionel did not see the implied meaning, and John took no notice of it, which confirmed both the doctor and Haidee in their suspicions of him. Sir Lionel merely replied:

"Of course your business is with me; but I have no secrets from Mr. John Trelawney.

John—you will be as surprised as I was—Dr. Mostyn assures me that Singleton is not mad."

" Indeed ! Do you consider his cure complete, Dr. Mostyn ? It must have been very rapid, for I saw you only two or three days ago, and you said he was not in a fit state to see me."

" Excuse me. I said he declined to see you," said the doctor. " Mr. Trelawney has never been mad at all."

John looked at Sir Lionel.

" Not mad !" said he. " Then—but I cannot believe that he is sane! at least, that he was sane when he—the night he left home."

" He is sane, and has never been insane. He denies having fired at his father, stating that at the time the shot was fired he was at a considerable distance. This he says he will prove, if set at liberty and given time."

Haidee looked up, and was about to say that John himself could prove the truth of her brother's assertion, when once again a warning glance from Dr. Mostyn silenced her.

John did not like this half-statement at all. It implied more than any open accusation, and embarrassed him sorely.

"What do you think, John?" Sir Lionel inquired. "Dr. Mostyn declines to keep him, and it seems that if I send him to another asylum Miss Trelawney will take legal proceedings against me. I presume my only course is to hand him over to the police, to stand his trial for firing at me. Yet I am unwilling to do this. I dislike the publicity."

"Well, dear Sir Lionel, if Dr. Mostyn is right in supposing that Singleton is sane, he will hardly attempt any repetition of the offence. I think you are quite safe, *if* he is sane."

"Safe—I was not thinking of that. Of course I can take precautions; but suppose he is *not* sane? On whom may his wrath fall next? And the disgrace — the scandal? I confess I deprecate the publicity that may ensue."

"Singleton has nothing to dread from publicity," remarked Haidee, with a slight emphasis upon her brother's name.

"Does he ask for a public trial?" inquired John, unable to repress the question, though he knew he had better not ask it.

"No," said Dr. Mostyn, "not yet. He is willing to try to convince his father privately, before invoking the aid of the law. This, not for his own sake. He would do much to spare his father's feelings."

" Indeed !" replied John, with a sneer. Quite a new idea, that; but I thought he would be in no hurry to call in the aid of the law."

" Then Mr. Trelawney may return home, Sir Lionel ?"

" I suppose so," he answered reluctantly. " I am not more cowardly than most men ; but I shall take precautions for the safety of the house. When will he arrive, Dr. Mostyn ?"

" Probably this evening. Perhaps, Miss Trelawney, you will drive over for him, or shall he come alone ?"

" I will meet him—tell him to be at the Royal at five o'clock, and I will call there for him."

" That will be the best way. Sir Lionel, I think my croydon is at the door; may I ring and inquire ?"

" Not yet; you must have some luncheon before you go," said Haidee, ringing the bell herself. Sir Lionel, entirely disapproving of her politeness to the objectionable physician, betook himself to his own apartments with a stately bow. John, quite exhausted by the agitation he had gone through, also departed, leaving Haidee and the doctor alone.

"Dr. Mostyn! how can I thank you? I hardly dared to hope for success; but you managed so beautifully and so quietly."

Dr. Mostyn smiled.

"I was half afraid you would be annoyed with me for having silenced you once or twice; but, indeed, Miss Trelawney, your impetuosity would have done harm. Now, I do hope that both you and your brother will be very prudent and careful. You will have a good deal to bear. I'm afraid Sir Lionel honestly believes what he asserts, and your cousin is a dangerous enemy. If your brother cannot govern his temper I really think he would do well to leave home for a time."

"He must find poor old James first, and prove his innocence," said Haidee, leading the way to the dining-room.

Soon afterwards the doctor drove away to gladden poor Singleton with his good news.

Haidee sent for Mrs. Thompson, and desired her to see that Mr. Trelawney's room was ready for him, as he would be at home by dinner-time. She pretended not to see the stout housekeeper's expression of dismay, nor the blank astonishment on the countenance of Pierce when she bid him order the carriage. "For I am going into Plymouth to meet Mr. Trelawney and bring him home," she said quietly.

For a moment Pierce thought that his dignity required him to give warning; but he refrained. Whether Singleton were mad or sane, the place was a good place, and not to be lightly lost.

CHAPTER II.

At the appointed time, Haidee Trelawney drove up to the door of the Royal Hotel. There was, as was usual, two or three persons, the porter, a stray waiter, and a man who looked like an ex-waiter, lounging about the door, and Haidee fancied that they exchanged significant glances when George inquired if Mr. Trelawney were in the hotel? The waiter came forward.

"Yes, Mr. Trelawney had been there nearly an hour."

Haidee looked out, and said:

"Tell him that I am here, if you please; say Miss Trelawney has called for him."

The man hurried away, and after a short time (during which the party at the door increased with such wonderful rapidity that there were soon twelve loungers instead of three), Singleton came out, followed by the waiter with his valise. Haidee could not doubt that the whole party had collected there to see Singleton, for they one and all stared and gaped after the manner of Englishmen when any person of note comes under their ken; but as Singleton himself did not appear to perceive it, she was careful to say nothing. He looked thin and ill, but brightened up wonderfully when he saw her, and in a few minutes they were on their way to the Abbey.

"Dear Singie! it is so lovely to see you sitting here beside me again. What a miserable time I have had of it, to be sure! And you even more miserable, my poor dear boy."

He looked at her thoughtfully for a moment or so, without speaking.

"Was it very dreadful, Singleton?"

"It was a time to be forgotten, if possible. But I shall never forget it. I've laid up a jolly good stock of material for bad dreams, *I* know. Haidee, it's no exaggeration to say that it would have made their assertion true if it had lasted long. I should have gone mad. Good heavens! the sounds I used to hear! The howls, the moans, and then to see them!"

"But you were not obliged to see them, I thought."

"I couldn't always help it. There is a

fellow there who went to sea at the same time that I did—a jolly little fellow, always larking and chaffing. He got fever of some kind and was sent home, and I thought no more of him until I saw him there. I heard an awful scrimmage under my window, and before I thought about it I ran to look out. There was poor little H——, as round and rosy a rollypolly as of old, with two keepers hard put to it to prevent him hurting himself, or them. And *such* a good little fellow he used to be—religious and all that, and now he was cursing them like—worse than Sir Lionel. Oh, I wish I hadn't seen him! I *cannot* forget it."

"Don't speak of it, dear—don't think of it," said Haidee softly, but he went on, not heeding her.

"And it is such a hopeless case, Mostyn tells me. His father died in a mad-house, and two more of them—his sisters—are mad too." He shuddered and turned pale as he spoke, and Haidee thought she had better change the subject, even if the new topic were an unpleasant one. So she said presently:

"I'm afraid, Singie dear, you'll find papa very hard to bear with. It is as well to warn you beforehand of that."

"Mostyn warned me, in a general way.

But can you give me any notion what line he'll take? Is he sure I'm mad, or what?"

"I don't know, indeed! I saw him only for a moment just as I was coming away. I went to his room to know if he had any message for Plymouth, and—" She hesitated.

"And what said he? Something fatherly and affectionate, or it would not be Sir Lionel."

"It was not anything he said to me."

"Well, what did he do then? Walk out of the room the moment you mentioned my name?"

"No, it was not that either. I may as well tell you, Singleton, for it will be your best way not to appear to observe it; he was giving orders to Ruskin, the carpenter, to see to all the fastenings and bolts of his rooms and windows, and to put heavy bolts outside the doors which shut off the west wing bedrooms. And one of the men is to sit up all night. And I saw a pair of pistols on the table, which he was loading."

Singleton stared at her for a moment; then threw himself back and laughed until his eyes were full of tears. That merry, boyish laugh! it was not often heard again. To their surprise the carriage was stopped, and George appeared at the window with a scared and anxious look.

"Did you call, Miss Trelawney?"

"No! what made you think I called? Is the check-string out of order?"

"No, ma'am, it is all right. I beg pardon, ma'am, but I thought I heard you call."

He disappeared, and with him disappeared Singleton's mirth. He looked grave and thoughtful for some time, and then said:

"I suppose he had been told to watch. I don't know how I can bear it, Haidee. It won't be very pleasant to be watched and dreaded like this."

"But you will soon prove that you did not do it, dear Singleton."

"I hope so; but remember that it all happened more than a month ago, and I have been locked up all that time, while John has been at liberty to do all he can to make it hard for me to find poor old James. However, come what will of it, Haidee, liberty is sweet! and I'm thankful I am not to eat my Christmas dinner in a mad-house. I shall take care they don't get me into one again."

"We must indeed. But that will not be difficult."

"Now, Haidee, tell me one thing, and tell me

the plain truth, for I would rather know it at once. How—what view does Reginald take of all this?"

Haidee looked anxiously at him.

"He was quite sure, Singie, that you never did this thing if you were yourself. I wrote to him yesterday evening, to say that I had found you."

"If I were myself! does that mean that he believed me to be mad?"

"Singleton, have patience, for my sake; remember how things looked. First came the story of your debts, which you refused to explain."

"But I said I could, and would, only not at once."

"Still, there it was, and then came the loss of the five hundred pounds, coupled with the firing at papa. And you were silent; not even a line to me; and your disappearance, which seemed to be your own act. I do think, Singleton, that you must not be too hard upon any one who was frightened and puzzled at all this."

"Yet this, and twenty times this, would not make me doubt him! and *you* did not doubt me, Haidee."

"Dear Singie, don't hate me! I did doubt,

as you know, about the debts—not the rest."

"But will he believe me now? that's the question. Will he accept my explanation, or believe John's denial? for of course he *will* deny it, and I have only my word to put against his, so far. There is one, though, who could bear witness that I told her the same story before any one else knew a word of it, except John and myself."

"Who is that?" then she added quickly, "Oh, Singie! did you tell Hester and not me?"

"Why, my dear girl, if I had told you, my whole fine plan would have been spoiled. You were the very person I could not tell. *She* warned me that I was playing with edged tools too; does she know how badly I cut myself?"

"I don't know what she knows, she has been away from home for some time. But I shall write it all to her now, Singie."

"Oh, *she'll* trust me, I have no doubt of her," answered Singleton absently. Haidee flushed up a little.

"You have no right, I think, to doubt Reginald. He will believe what I believe."

"Perhaps so; but he's much more likely to want you to believe what he believes."

"Why should you say that? I don't think you are quite kind, Singleton."

"My dear, I don't mean anything unkind, either of him, or to you. You know how I love and admire him; but I do know, to be frank with you, that when he has expressed an opinion he is very slow to change it."

"Well, we shall see. I don't think you do him justice; he'll be only too glad to hear the truth. But we are just at home, and I must have one word as to our plans. I hope you will not enter upon any explanations with Sir Lionel until you can prove to him that you did not fire that shot. Then he will believe the rest—at least it will be possible to make him listen. Just now he believes no one but John."

"That's Mostyn's advice too. He says it all hangs upon that—find old James, and the rest is clear, particularly as John was actually with me when we heard the shot! By the way, does that gallant officer *never* put in a little service? His colonel must be the most indulgent of men, don't you think?"

"I wish he were not, then. It's too bad having him always watching and crawling about, and that wretch Phillips is just as bad. But you mean, then, to say nothing just yet?"

"Nothing. I shall have advice at once. Mr. Seldon, I think. Here we are now. Hallo, Pierce, is that you?"

"I hope I see you well, Mr. Trelawney," said Pierce nervously, watching Singleton in a way which inspired Haidee with an insane desire to throw her muff at him.

"My old room, I suppose? Send up my traps, Pierce. Dinner at eight, Haidee? All right, I shall be in time;" then in a whisper, "I shan't go to my father; we had better meet before witnesses, I think."

"Yes, I shall take care to be down before you."

When father and son met, which they did in the drawing-room a few minutes before eight, Sir Lionel merely bowed, as if to a perfect stranger. Singleton, with a glance at Haidee half amused, half angry, imitated his distant demeanour. But when John advanced with outstretched hand, he drew back.

"No, John. It's war to the knife between us now, and you must expect no more mercy than you showed me."

Sir Lionel was looking on, so John was obliged to, as it were, take up the glove.

"As you will—but in the meantime, we should not be the worse for shaking hands, should we?"

"You would not. I should," answered Singleton quietly. Sir Lionel and John looked at each other and raised their eyebrows. Dinner was announced.

"Take in your cousin, John," said Sir Lionel; but Haidee, though doubtful of the wisdom of her brother's frankness, would not even seem to side with the enemy, so she took his arm and marched him off, leaving the others to follow as they liked.

Next day, after breakfast, Haidee and Singleton sent for Pierce, and asked him to go over the oft-told tale of the shot from the evergreens. Pierce was unwilling and embarrassed, requiring no small amount of questioning before it became quite clear what he had seen and what he had only conjectured. Singleton wrote down his statement, and read it over to him.

"Is that correct, Pierce?"

"Quite so, sir."

"Very good. Thank you, that's all I want of you at present. If it was worth my while to argue the matter with a fellow who could take up *such* an idea with so little reason, I should ask you what, in the name of common sense, made you conclude that I was the person you saw? You saw a man run, not very quick you say, and scramble through the hedge. Whereas I am a rather good runner, and you must have seen me run and clear that hedge at a bound about a hundred times while I was at home."

"Not since you was hill, sir."

"Yes, since I was ill. It's nothing of a jump, you know."

"I'm sure I don't know, sir; I am no jumper myself. But it was Sir Lionel as said it were you, sir, to the best of my belief."

"Oh! and you did not think it was me until he said so?"

"I really believe I did not, sir—I hadn't time to think. But the Scotch cap went a great way, no doubt."

"No doubt it did. And I hope you'll like the fool's cap which I shall make you a present of by-and-by. Well, that's all, Pierce."

The man withdrew, looking almost as foolish as if he already wore the ornamental headdress so kindly promised him.

"Now, Haidee, I'm going into Plymouth. The ship was the *Stars and Stripes*, bound for New York, eh? I hope I may be able to find out that James did not sail: poor old James, I feel half ashamed of trying to fix it on him."

"But it was surely his act. I think—Oh, Singie, no one would punish him much! he was never quite sensible, and latterly was often very strange."

"Drank—that's the English of it, my child : well, good-bye, my dear. I am gone."

Haidee was on the watch for his return, and met him as he rode slowly to the door.

"Well, Singie! any news?" she cried cheerily, trying not to believe her eyes as to his dejected look. He dismounted and stood before her, watching her face earnestly while he spoke.

"Haidee, the *Stars and Stripes* sailed on the evening of that day—the day James went on board."

"Then where can he be now! I wonder has he left England yet?"

To her surprise, Singleton covered his face with his hand and said in a tone of the deepest earnestness:

"Thank God, my prayer *was* heard then."

"Your prayer! what prayer?"

"The very first I ever made, I think. Oh, Haidee, I did so dread seeing in your eyes that this staggered even you. I have been praying all the way home that you might trust me still."

"You foolish, poor dear boy! as if I *could* be such a donkey. But did you make any further inquiries? Has no one seen him since that evening?"

"No one, that I could make out. I went to all the places our servants are known at : but if he had made up his poor crazy mind to shoot Sir Lionel, he would have kept himself out of the way as much as possible."

"He cannot have come on purpose to do it, Singleton ; for the gun, you know, was lying there, which he could not have known. It seems to me far more likely that he came to make a last appeal, and finding the gun, was tempted, poor old man. Well, Singie! all is not lost because not won to-day : what do you think of—Here's a carriage—a cab, is it not ? who can it be ?"

They drew to one side to let the cab pass them, and Haidee saw that the occupant was Reginald Hamilton.

"Why, I declare it is Regie!" she cried joyously. "He must have come off as soon as he got my letter. Now all will be comfortable! we shall soon make him understand everything."

They went on after the cab, Singleton leading his horse : and in the porch they met Reginald.

"Why, Regie! this is a pleasant surprise," Haidee said, holding out her two little hands to him.

He took them, and held them affectionately, but looked beyond her all the time.

"Is that Singleton?" he asked in a low voice.

"Yes—you had my letter this morning I suppose?"

"Oh yes, I came off at once."

A servant had now taken Singleton's horse, and set him free to come forward, which he did slowly, with a somewhat anxious look from one to the other. Reginald shook hands with him, and probably a stranger would have noticed nothing amiss in his manner. But after a few moments of exceedingly awkward silence, Singleton turned away suddenly and went into the house. Reginald looked after him.

"He looks very, very ill, Haidee. So pale and worn."

"He does: but a few days will set him up again."

"And how do you think him — in other ways? but I suppose you can hardly judge yet."

Haidee looked thoughtfully at him. Then she, too, turned to enter the house, saying with a slight shiver:

"It has grown so cold! I am frozen. Pierce, send tea to the drawing-room, I suppose there is a good fire there. Are you hungry, Reginald, or will a cup of tea satisfy you?"

"I am not hungry, thank you."

"Tell Mrs. Thompson to put Mr. Hamilton in one of the south rooms, Pierce. Any of them will do."

"Not in my old quarters, Haidee?"

She made no answer, but led the way to the drawing-room, and threw her hat and fur jacket on a sofa.

"Reginald, what did you mean by your question about Singleton?"

"I meant to ask, do you think he is quite himself now?"

"He is quite himself and has never been otherwise. Dr. Mostyn told papa so, and would not keep him in his asylum, because he was not, nor ever had been, out of his mind."

"So you said in your letter. I was very much surprised."

"And pleased, Regie?"

He was silent.

"Oh, Regie! why—what is this?"

"I *cannot* account for his conduct, if he were sane all along, Haidee."

"But I told you how he explains his debts? did you not read that?"

"I did; I must inquire, speak to John Trelawney about it. It is a story so utterly wild that it sounds more like the raving of an unsettled intellect than a narrative of facts. Have you, or has Dr. Mostyn, tested the truth of it in any way?"

"No. In fact Singleton never told that part of his story to Dr. Mostyn until the doctor had pronounced him sane on other grounds. And as to asking John, I neither have done so, nor shall do it. A lie comes as readily to John's lips as words do. But, Reginald, Singleton told the same story to one person, before it was wanted as a defence. To Hester, while you were all staying here."

"I know he did. Part of it, but not all. There is now something about an additional debt."

"But that happened since then. Don't you see that he could not have told Hester unless it were true?"

Again no answer. "Oh! Reginald dear, surely you see that?"

"No, Haidee. He wanted her to think well of him and knew that he must ask his father for the money. He did not tell you, because you would have told me: and only an innocent, guileless girl was likely to believe his story."

"And yet you think him mad! No madman would have thought of that."

"A great amount of cunning goes with madness: but upon my conscience, if you are right in thinking him sane, I don't know what to think."

Haidee's eyes flashed, and angry words rose to her lips: but she checked herself, and burst into tears. He came to her side, laid a gentle, loving hand upon hers and said, "My poor Haidee! It is very dreadful for you."

Haidee sprang up, dried her eyes, and said quickly, "I hear his step—answer me one question at once. What does Hester say?"

"She believes only what he told her."

Before she could reply, Singleton came in by one door and the servants with tea by another. They drank tea in a very silent and uncomfortable way, poor Haidee making gallant but unsuccessful efforts to get up a conversation; and presently Reginald said he would go to his room. Singleton watched him with wistful eyes, and when he had shut the door, he sighed deeply. Haidee came to him and kissed him.

"My dear, kind Haidee! I have but thing to ask of you. *Don't* quarrel with him on my account, my dear."

"That's easy to say, Singleton. But you were my brother before I ever saw him—you and I are only just two, and we must hold

3—2

together. If I deserted you for him I should never know a moment's happiness again."

"But there is no question of desertion in the matter, Impetuosity. Sooner or later the truth will come out, and then all will be right. But I am very anxious that you should not have words with him about it—or about me. You will never convince him! never, if he has once made up his mind. And you would not find it easy to make up with him again."

"Oh, it won't come to that. We are too fond of each other."

"My dear girl, don't run any risk of it. Just let the question alone—time will settle it. I assure you Reginald is not a person to trifle with. He has a thousand noble qualities—he's as fine a fellow as ever walked a deck; but he's one with whom you quarrel only once."

"I cannot think thus of him."

"You may believe me. Once, and once only. It is not as with me, a flash and then forget it. You know only the soft side of him, but there is a hard one too, remember. And yet I don't know any one I should so gladly see you married to, Haidee, except my dear old captain, and *he* is not likely to think of you."

"Well, no," she answered with a laugh, "that *would* be rather too much, I think. I will be careful, Singie, believe me. Now if you were to follow him to his room and have a quiet talk with him, I think it might do good."

"I mean to go. But first tell me, Hester—I mean, has she told him that she knew all this?"

"Yes: and she believes you firmly. Now, go, dear, and make him hear the whole story from beginning to end."

Singleton went. But he lost some time by going first to Reginald's old room near his own, and it was some time before he found out where he was now. He saw George coming out of a room in the distance, and called to him.

"George! I say, George! where have they put Mr. Hamilton?"

"In here, sir. The Red room."

"I want to speak to him. He's in his room, I suppose?" said Singleton, walking down the passage.

"No, sir. I have just shown him the way to the Captain's room downstairs."

Singleton started a little, but said nothing. He went into the Red room, which looked very cheery in the firelight, and sat down by the fire.

"The Captain's room," he muttered. "I have a great mind to go down and confront John—but no; there would be a row, and it would be used against me. Half-past six—he will be back presently. I shall wait for him."

But he waited more than an hour before Reginald came, and during that time his mood changed considerably. He came there, prepared to make an appeal to their long friendship—to the new bond between them; and to tell him the whole story "from beginning to end" as Haidee had said. But as the slow minutes passed, while Hamilton was still closeted with John, is it to be wondered at that poor Singleton's temper began to rise, and a bitter feeling to take possession of him? At last the door opened, and Reginald came in, looking stern and grave, Singleton thought—but he would make one effort, if only for Haidee's sake.

" I've been waiting here this hour and more for you, Reginald. But you have been a long time with John."

" I did not know that you were here, or that you wanted me."

" No. Nor did I know, when I came here, that you would seek an explanation of things that have been going on from John Trelawney —my bitterest enemy. Was that the act of a friend? of one soon to be a brother?"

" I did not mean it as an unfriendly act, Singleton. I had a hope that I might clear up some difficulties; there were questions which I wished to ask—which none but he could answer."

"Ay! and what were they? but you need not tell me; I know. You asked whether it were true that I had paid eight thousand pounds for John—and he denied it stoutly, of course."

"He says he assisted you to get the money, which he now deeply regrets."

"Of course he does: deeply. And you believe him implicitly, of course?"

"Singleton, have you any papers—receipts—to prove that the money was paid on his account?"

"None. He's not such a fool as to let that happen. Well—and that decides you that I am —romancing?"

"It's a very—wild—and improbable story, Singleton."

"It is indeed: very wild as you say—incredible to the last degree. The notion that any man could get himself into such a mess, merely to secure, as he hoped, the happiness of his sister and his friend, is absurd—isn't it? *You* would never have been so foolish, that seems quite clear. But, my dear fellow, you might not have found my father quite so easy to deal with if I had been as cool and sensible as you would have been."

Hamilton coloured and threw back his head. "Having gained Haidee's love," he said coldly, "Sir Lionel's consent must needs have followed. The days when women could be coerced in this matter are gone by, as every man in his senses knows."

The expression escaped him unawares, but Singleton naturally enough thought he meant it literally.

"I see," said he. "If I were in my senses, I should not have thought my interference necessary. So if I'm telling the truth I'm a madman, and if I'm telling a lie I'm a scoundrel, and a murderer. All right. We'll say no more about it. Look here, Hamilton! for Haidee's sake we must not quarrel. I am going up to town to-morrow to get advice, so I shan't be in your way long. Good-bye for the present, there isn't time to do more than dress for dinner now. You don't object to dine at the same table with me, do you? The knives, you know. It might be awkward. You don't?—very good. Farewell until then."

He rushed back to his room in such a storm of sorrow and anger, that it was some time before he could calm himself enough to change his dress, and dinner was half over before he appeared.

Haidee knew by his face that the interview with Hamilton had not been pleasant, and fully intended to know all about it before she slept, but he successfully avoided her all that evening, and in the early morning appeared by her bedside, with only time (so he declared) to kiss her and run away, if he meant to catch the early train for town."

"But, oh! Singleton," Haidee exclaimed, rubbing her sleepy eyes and blinking at his candle, only half awake, "I had fifty questions to ask you, and a great deal of good advice to give you—you have no business to run away like this."

"Must, my dear. Apologise for me to Sir Lionel: say it was a sudden resolution. Don't be afraid, Haidee, I shall take care of myself, for all our sakes; and the less you have to say to me the better for yourself. So good-bye—I'm off."

But Haidee, wide awake now, sprung from her bed and caught him.

"Promise me—on your honour—that you'll come back. If you don't promise, I'll—I'll follow you, Singleton, by the next train."

"I will come back, I promise."

"Whatever happens?—and whether you like it or not?"

"You imperious young woman! Yes, my dear," kissing her lovingly, "I will come back, indeed. Now get back into bed, or you'll have your death of cold. Good-bye, Haidee." He went to the door, but then came back to say, "Haidee, I entreat you not to have words with Hamilton about me. Leave it alone until I come home."

Then the door closed, and he was gone.

"Like a flash of lightning," Haidee murmured, as she crept shivering back into her bed; "*too* bad to have come when I was only half awake like this."

However he was gone, and there was nothing to be done but to wait until he came back again.

CHAPTER III.

So Haidee and her lover were together again, with no one to interfere in their lives; for Sir Lionel and John kept much together, and away from them. Only a little while ago they would have asked nothing more of fate; but now, alas! there was no pleasure in it. There was something wrong; it began even on that first morning, when Haidee informed Reginald of Singleton's departure for London, and that he had begged that his affairs might not be discussed until his return. To her great annoyance, Reginald's first impulse was to follow him by the next train.

"I came here to take care of you," said he; "but he will try to see Hester, and I ought to be at home."

"I am glad you came, for any reason, Regie; but I don't at all need to be taken care of. I should think that mamma and Mr. Hamilton were quite able to look after Hester without your help, and I tell you plainly that if you leave me now, I shall be very angry; but you must do as you like."

She walked away, giving him no time to answer; but he stayed, of course. Perhaps, however angry she might have been, it would have been wiser of him to go; for the natural consequence of their determination not to speak of that which filled their hearts and minds, was that they had neither pleasure nor comfort in being together. Instead of the old happy talks and delightful silences, they now laboriously "made conversation" when alone with each other, and were conscious of a feeling of relief when Sir Lionel or John was present. The days dragged slowly on, that used to fly; and the worst of it was, that poor impetuous Haidee could not always keep her resolution to be silent about her brother, but spoke her mind with considerable vigour and freedom when any chance occasion roused her indignation afresh, and only remembered the said resolution when Reginald attempted a reply, when she used it to crush him promptly—a piece of womanly injustice which fretted him much, though he was outwardly calm. Then she thought that his calmness denoted want of feeling, and that fretted her, so that she spoke with added bitterness when next they fell out. The truth was, that the wide difference between their dispositions and tempers was making itself felt, and neither of them was in a position to take the upper hand. If they had been man and wife, Haidee's good principles would have made her submit; and perhaps Reginald, if his authority had been secure, would not have cared to exercise it. As matters actually stood, he felt that she was taking an unfair advantage of him. Haidee, passionate and frank, said all that she meant and a great deal more; fancying that he, because he was calm and silent, did not care about it. Reginald, unused to such plain speaking, thought that she meant all that she said, and a great deal more; and remembered every word when poor Impetuosity had forgotten it. It was the old story: the story of "the little rift within the lute," and already the sweet music of love and trust was silenced.

On the fourth day after his departure, Singleton appeared at the dinner-table.

"Why, Singie! I did not know you were come back."

"I only came about half an hour ago, and you were gone to your room. I beg your pardon,

Sir Lionel, for being so late; I really could not help it. Well, Hamilton! you have had fine weather for rides and walks. Have you been out much?"

Nothing of any importance passed during dinner; but as he opened the door for Haidee to leave the room, he whispered: "Go to your own room, and I will follow presently." Then he went back to the table, and standing beside it, addressed his father:

"Sir Lionel, I sent a message, requesting leave to speak to you in your own room before dinner. You refused to see me; but I hope you will let me say a few words to you now."

"You may speak," replied Sir Lionel, with even more than his ordinary stiff frigidity.

"I went to the Admiralty while I was in town, to ask them to send me to sea. I was told that I had been appointed to the *Endymion*, Captain Hamilton's ship, and that my appointment had been cancelled, by your desire; and I think you told them that I was mad and in confinement, although, of course, they did not like to say so plainly. Did you do this?"

"I did tell him so. I saw the Duke of——" (naming the First Lord) "and told him so."

"But as you are now aware that I am not

mad, will you write and say so? for if you do not, I fear I shall never get employed again."

"Certainly I shall not. I confess myself amazed at your audacity in preferring such a request. Dr. Mostyn assures me that you are not mad, but his is, after all, but the unsupported opinion of a third-rate practitioner. The fact that you attempted my life, not to mention other matters, remains: and I can only say that I hope you had the excuse of insanity."

"I have put that matter into good hands, and sooner or later it will be cleared up. In the meantime, I am advised to ask you to listen to a brief statement—or rather explanation of many things in my conduct which must have appeared strange to you—and others," with a glance at Reginald. "I have it here in writing, and I'm going to read it to you, and then I shall leave it with you. I don't myself expect *you* to believe it, Sir Lionel; but I suppose it is right that you should hear my side of the story."

"You may read it, but you are right in concluding that I shall attach little importance to anything you can say."

Thus encouraged, Singleton unfolded a paper which he drew from his pocket, and read a clear, concise, and well-considered statement of the circumstances which had appeared so extraordinary. As I have already given a full account of all, I need not go over them now. In spite of the unsympathising silence of his audience, he read it every word, distinctly accusing John of being well aware that whoever fired at Sir Lionel, it was not his son, and also giving a plain account of the money transactions between them, so far as he had positive knowledge of them, but merely denying the theft of the notes without attempting to fix it upon the real culprit. Then he folded the paper up and gave it to his father.

"Keep it, father. It may well be that I shall be in my grave before the proofs of my story come to light. But when they do, I know that, dead or alive, you will do me justice. I have been locked up, and my enemy free, and he has made it very hard to find the proofs I want; but they'll come out some day, of that you may be certain."

He spoke to his father and to John, but his wistful eyes were fixed on Reginald's face. Sir Lionel took up the paper.

"I shall keep it as you say. I look upon it as the completed proof of your insanity. I do not believe that any one in the possession of an unclouded intelligence would expect any one to believe that story about the money. When John informed me that you had made such a statement, I——"

"John informed you?" exclaimed Singleton, his face brightening, "How did he know it? I have never spoken to him since I left Dr. Mostyn's."

"Mr. Hamilton was my informant. I concluded he had it from you," replied John.

Singleton glanced quickly at Hamilton, and said:

"I understand—never mind, Reginald, it does not matter. I interrupted you, Sir Lionel—I beg your pardon."

Sir Lionel bowed majestically, but did not resume his discourse. After waiting some moments in vain, Singleton spoke again.

"Then, Sir Lionel, you don't believe a word I have said: and you won't write to the Admiralty."

"You are correct in both statements."

"Then I have no more to say; but I don't believe that God will let such villany go unpunished. Reginald, come out here, I want to speak to you."

"Singleton," said John Trelawney, as his cousin turned to leave the room, "I don't know that it is necessary for me to speak, but you understand that I utterly deny the frantic accusations you have made against me. I never profited by the money transactions in London; that I assisted you in any way I now deeply regret; but I did it for your father's sake. I did not meet you on the day Sir Lionel was fired at; and I am unwillingly obliged to add, that a hope having entered my mind that Black James might have been the culprit, I took some trouble to ascertain that the negro sailed for New York the day before."

Singleton took no notice of the speaker, even by a look, and in the midst of the speech he quietly left the room: Reginald following in a moment more. They went into the gallery.

"Hamilton," exclaimed Singleton, in a voice so tender, so imploring, so changed from that in which he had spoken to his father, that one could hardly believe it was the same person who spoke. "Regie! you know now all that I can say. The only proof of my truth which I can offer—and I could not offer it to *them*—is, that I told the same story to Hester before any one else knew anything about it. Reginald, you've known me for years; I have had no secrets from you. You must know that I could not be guilty of such deeds as these. Say that *you* trust me, and I can wait patiently until I can prove it to the rest of the world."

Reginald looked at him—pale and agitated.

"I don't know how to answer you," he said. "If you yourself believe the story you have just told in there, why did you not take the one step which would have proved that you did believe it? I waited, expecting every moment that you would say: 'I demand as an act of justice that you accuse me publicly of this crime, and let me prove my innocence.' But you never hinted at it."

"That is not my doing—I wanted to do that very thing, but have been advised not. I have had legal advice, and considering the difficulty there seems likely to be in finding Black James, and that he is the only witness—not witness either, but evidence rather, that will establish my innocence, as John won't—I was overruled, and advised to wait."

Hamilton was silent.

"Reginald! won't you trust me? Both Haidee and Hester——"

"Stop there," Reginald interrupted him sternly. "There is no occasion to bring my sister's name in the affair at all. Haidee believes you, you would say. I know she does. And cold and unfeeling as she calls me, I would give all I have or hope to have in the world, to believe as she does. But I cannot! your story is wild—improbable—nearly impossible in fact; unsupported, except by your own assertions. I really don't know how she contrives to believe it."

"Do you conclude, then, that I don't believe it myself?" asked Singleton; his voice and manner changing—hardening with every word.

Reginald turned and looked at him doubtfully.

"*Do* you believe it, Singleton?" he asked gravely.

Singleton laughed—one of the reckless, bitter laughs which Haidee hated to hear.

"Have it as you like!" he said. "To a friend—a friend in *my* sense of the word, I would answer any question; to an inquisitor trying to catch me out and get evidence to prove me mad out of my own mouth, I shan't answer at all. Well—that's over; let us say no more about it. Hamilton, Haidee loves you; and I am not going to stand in the way of her happiness. I am going away soon. You will see little more of me until matters are somewhat different. I am going to Haidee now, and shall not come down again, so good-night—and farewell."

CHAPTER IV.

"I THOUGHT you were never coming, Singie! what has kept you so long?"

"I wanted to speak to Sir Lionel, and it took some time."

"Well—now that you *have* come, sit down, and tell me all about everything. Sit here in this comfortable chair; you look so tired and weary, my own poor boy."

He sat down as directed, drew her towards him and kissed her fondly; then gazed absently into the fire and let her stroke the wavy hair off his forehead and otherwise pet him for some time. Then he started, and asked:

"What o'clock is it, Haidee? That was ten striking, wasn't it? yes. Look here, my dear. Send down word that you won't reappear to-night. I want to have you all to myself just this once. Are you sleepy? shall you mind sitting up some time?"

"Not at all—but I may as well send Anne to bed. I can do without her."

"No, no—we may want her. Good old Anne, she is one of the few we can trust entirely, and I know she won't grudge a little trouble for us."

"That she won't. Well—now, Singie, I am ready. I have nothing to do now but listen to you: and I am very anxious to know what you have been doing, and what you had to say to Sir Lionel."

"I shall tell you everything, my dear: but the plain fact is easily told in few words. I am a ruined man. I haven't a thing left on the face of the earth that I care for, except the love of two dear good girls; and one of them is kept from me, and from the other I must run away!"

"No, you shan't, Singleton!"

"You won't say so when you've heard all."

"Did you see—Hester?"

"No. I went there, and asked for Mrs. Hamilton. She came at once: but alone. She was very kind, but dreadfully embarrassed, poor thing. I told her I came because as Hester had mentioned that she knew my story, I thought it more straightforward to come forward at once: that I loved her, and thought she loved me: and that when I had cleared myself from actual charges, I hoped they would not let Sir Lionel's assertion that I was mad influence them. She sent for Mr. Hamilton then—and nothing could be kinder than they both were."

"They promised what you asked, then?"

"No, they did not. I hardly thought they could, you know. With—Reginald against me—but indeed they did not bring in his name. They said Hester was very young and they would allow no promise of any kind. Mr. Hamilton said he must speak plainly—that the whole affair was very mysterious, and he really did not know what to think, but that if I could prove myself quite innocent, and that matters really had happened as I asserted, they would think the matter over—as regarded Hester I mean."

"And was that all?"

"All. I asked to see her, but they refused. I don't think she was in the house. Mrs. Hamilton said I was much to blame for having spoken to her as I did, without their leave. I know I was. I see it now."

"*I* don't! Hester's as old as I am, very nearly—and twice as wise. Well, what next?"

"I asked plainly if he would refuse her to me if I proved that I did not fire at Sir Lionel; would they take that as proof of my innocence, and of the truth of my story. He said he would not bind himself to anything : that he would be guided by circumstances. In fact, I suppose he feels that he can't be sure I'm not mad : so one must not blame him."

" I suppose not—but why should they refuse to believe Dr. Mostyn ?"

" Well—they didn't refuse. They did not say anything more than I have told you. Then I went to Mr. Seldon. He was here you know, when I told my father about the money. To him I told the whole affair—you must know he and I had become very friendly while he was here, and though he is Sir Lionel's solicitor, I felt he would understand me better than a stranger would. Bless me, how he questioned me! I felt like that "tender young cork" that Dickens speaks of somewhere, with a big corkscrew at work upon me. Then he asked me to dine with him next day, and he would think it over in the meantime."

" Then he was kind ? He believed you ?"

" More than kind. Oh, yes, he believed me— at once. He said he suspected something about John when he was here. Well, next day I went to the Admiralty, thinking I might as well go to sea for a while. There I found that my appointment to Captain Hamilton's ship had been cancelled in consequence of " representations " made by my father. In plain English, my dear, he had actually seen the Duke and told him I was mad, and in an asylum—and of course they all believed it, that was natural enough."

" My dear, dear, Singie; what a trial! what did you say ?"

" I stared like a cassowary, and said little or nothing. How can a fellow say, ' Please your grace, my father's a pompous old idiot, and I'm no more mad than you are.' I tried to insinuate that there had been a mistake—but the Duke said perhaps in that case, Sir Lionel would write to him. Then he bowed me out."

" But Sir Lionel will write, surely. He cannot be so cruel as to stop your career as a sailor, when——"

"When he's left me nothing else? Yes he can be so cruel. He won't write a line; I asked him."

Haidee sighed.

" I hope I may not come to hating him!" said she slowly.

" No no! He's hard—cold—what you will—but he's honest. He believes it himself, that makes all the difference. Well—to go on. I suspect Mr. John has been publishing his version of affairs industriously : but whether it was he or Sir Lionel I don't know, the result is the same. Nearly every one cut me; or looked as if they would if they could. Fellows I know quite well pretended not to see me: even a brother officer or two at the Admiralty hurried away with a bow."

"My poor Singleton! what a set of——"

"Not a bit—very natural. I pounced upon one fellow, and made him tell me what he had heard, and upon my word I should cut my twin brother if such things were true of him. I assured Vernon that it was all false, and he tried to look as if he believed me, and told me not to excite myself! Then I went to Mr. Seldon."

"And what advice does he give?"

"He advised me to leave England. He'll make my interest his own he says, and will work hard for me. But he thinks I'm not safe here. He had a letter from Sir Lionel that morning, asking him to tell him what legal steps were necessary for putting me in confinement; and he had written to say he thought it could not be done, as I seemed sane enough, having been with him about it all. But of course that will merely make Sir Lionel go elsewhere for help, and I am really not safe for a day, here. John must have some scheme in hand—we interrupted him by my escape from Mostyn's, but he won't give it up. This very moment I have little doubt they are busy devising means for getting me into some place or other; and I might not find another Mostyn, even if I had time given me."

"Time! how do you mean?"

"Why upon my word, Haidee, I think John must have had some notion of getting rid of me finally when he tried to send that creeping Phillips to attend upon me. Besides, I might go mad. I don't think any man's brains would stand a mad-house long. Seldon wanted me to go to sea—but I told him how matters stood about that: then he told me to go abroad for a while, and keep out of harm's way until he has found James and convinced my father, which he will leave no stone unturned to do. I can trust Seldon—entirely: and I mean to take his advice. I want your help, Haidee."

"Singleton—you are keeping back your true reason. You think that if you are away, there will be less danger of a quarrel between Reginald and me."

"A quarrel between you two, about me, would go near breaking my heart. I confess that. For although I cannot deny that I am surprised and hurt—yet I know he is a good fellow and will make you happy. And you'll want protection if I am to be kept away from England, and John living here, as he will be; for you'll find he will never dare to be off duty —I mean to let Sir Lionel out of his sight, for a day now. But Seldon thinks so strongly that I am not safe here, that he was very much against my coming back, even for a few hours. He says we may find it very hard to get hold of Black James. Heaven knows where the poor old man may be—but I would not be surprised if John knew—and if so he'll keep him out of our reach. As to the money matters, as I was such a fool as to allow John to destroy all papers, and all evidence, why the only thing to do is to wait till we can prove his falsehood about James, and then frighten him into confessing: or bribe him. He means to try and get hold of Phillips and see if he would turn informer."

"But surely you could help in all this Singie?" said poor Haidee.

"If I am locked up in a madhouse? or quietly poisoned? By George, Haidee that sounds absurd, but such things do happen, even in these days, and I assure you I think John is capable of anything. And that fellow would be a ready tool. I promised Seldon I would go at once."

"And Hester?"

"I shall write to Hester and you must send the letter open to Mrs. Hamilton. Oh, don't cry, my darling, and make it too hard for me, but help me. For I *must* go, Haidee."

"Yes," she said, crying bitterly, "you must, dear. I see it, and I will not be selfish."

"Why I read a statement of my version of the story to Sir Lionel to-night (by Seldon's advice), and he told me plainly he thought it a convincing proof of my insanity. And Hamilton thought so too, I think—at least he asked me if I believed it myself. Oh, if Sir Lionel wants to lock me up, he will find plenty to help him, they all think I should be a good riddance."

Haidee sprang up, her eyes flashing.

"If Reginald did that! I should never see his face again!"

"Ah, Haidee! you only convince me more than ever that I must go, if I don't want to be the cause of endless mischief. I am going this very night. I have a cab coming from Plymouth, in time for a train which will enable me to catch the Indian mail at Southampton. And I want you to help me to pack, and get away quietly. You did that once before, Haidee."

"To-night—must you go to-night?"

"Haidee, I only came back because of my promise to you! I am as certain as if I heard them, that Sir Lionel and John are at this moment laying their plans for getting me off to some asylum. You should have seen the look they gave each other when he said the paper was a proof of my insanity; and once locked up I should probably be really mad before you could get me out again."

"But where are you going? Oh, Singie, you *won't* leave me uncertain! You will write to me?"

"Of course I shall! I'm going to Captain Hamilton. I think he will stick to me. You see he knows something of my father, and so does Seldon; that gives me an advantage. Now Reginald does not know him as he is, at all; and you might talk for ever, and he would never understand. He's one that must see with his own eyes, not with yours. He has no notion what a fool Sir Lionel is—that sententious way of speaking deceives people."

Haidee shook her head.

"It is kind—and just like you, to make excuses for him, but——"

"Oh, you'll be all right when I am safe out of the way, my dear. And even if no harm came of it otherwise, I should be wretched if my presence made a coldness between you. Only keep things quiet, Haidee. The truth *must* come out, and then no one will be more sorry than Reginald."

"Sorry—how do you mean?"

"That he doubted me. Of course he'll be glad enough to believe it's all right. Come now, to my room and help me. I don't like to be alone in this house."

She found that he had nearly finished packing before dinner, and while she was putting up the rest of his goods, he went to his writing table to write to Hester. He opened the blotter.

"Hullo! what have we here? Miss Trelawney—why this must have been here ever so long, I must have forgotten to post it."

"Give it to me now, Singie."

It was the second letter written on the eventful day, when Sir Lionel was wounded. Written, because a harsh and angry one had been posted before he came to his senses, and went to recall it. Haidee understood this at a glance.

"Ah, if I had got this, it would have been such a comfort to me, Singleton."

"What's it all about? I suppose I forgot to post it."

Then he went on writing, and Haidee cried quietly over the affectionate, penitent words, which had been hid away from her until they were of no use: but not valueless, for she put them away with tender care.

Singleton wrote a few lines to his father, saying that Haidee would always know where he was; and the following letter to Hester, which he sent open in a cover to Mr. Hamilton.

"My Dear Hester,

"Your father tells me that I had no right to speak to you as I did without his leave. You know what my reasons were, but I acknowledge that he is right. I have ruined my own prospects (for the time at least), by those foolish proceedings which I confided to you, and against which you warned me. I would give worlds to know that I had not also made you unhappy.

"I am leaving England, by my kind friend Mr. Seldon's advice, until we can clear up the mystery that now darkens my name. I leave the matter in good hands, but it may so happen that we never shall find poor old foolish James, and till we do, it seems that my chance of being righted in the eyes of the world is but small.

"So I write, Hester, to say— and what it costs me I cannot tell you—and I hope you cannot imagine—but it must be said. I hope you will forget me. You are so young, that you may meet some one whom you will love as I once hoped to make you love me; and when that happens, let no thought of me disturb your happiness. I would rather, believe me, know that you were happy than know that you were still thinking of one so little worthy of you as I am, take me at my best; and now with nothing but my love to give you. That I love you truly, do not doubt. If I loved you less, I should ask you to remember me. Forgive me, dear Hester, for having selfishly brought you under the shadow of the dark cloud which my folly has brought down upon my life. Think of me and pray for me as for a brother, or at least as for one who cares more for your happiness than for his own.

"You see I do not assert my innocence. I know there is no need. And now good-bye, to you and home and all that makes life dear. I have been a great fool. God bless you, my Hester, that never may be mine.

"SINGLETON TRELAWNEY."

By the time the letter was written, Haidee had packed up all his possessions, and having summoned Anne to her aid, had got him some supper.

"Singleton, have you plenty of money?"

"Enough for the present. I suppose Sir Lionel won't stop my allowance, and at all events I can't starve, you know. Now that I'm a lieutenant there is my half pay. Were you going to offer me your purse, Haidee? Do you remember running down that great echoing staircase to give me all your little hoard, the time I ran away to go to sea?"

"I was going to say I wish it was not so empty. I paid for all my wedding finery," she said with a sigh, "before I left London."

"I assure you I don't want it just now. I will let you know if I am run short at any time. Here's my letter, and this for Sir Lionel; or shall I leave it for the servants to give to him?"

"No, give it to me."

"Now, if Anne would lend me a hand with these boxes, I should get them down into the porch. The conveyance must be here soon."

Anne helped with good will and many tears; she was a soft-hearted and rather timid woman, and was frightened out of her senses by the strange sounds the great empty house seemed full of in the quiet night.

" Now there's only this bag—the cab's come, Haidee. Come down to the door and see me off, if you're not afraid of the cold. Put your shawl over your head. Last time I did this —seems to me I'm always running away—do you know I walked right into John's trap? and my nerves have not got over it yet."

The cab, piled with trunks and bags, was ready to start when they reached the door.

" Good-bye, Anne—thank you for helping me. Take care of your mistress, Anne, she'll need it. Now Haidee," throwing his arms round her, "my dear good loving sister—good-bye."

" Not for long—I hope and trust," she tried to say.

" God grant it! but you'll be a married woman before I see you again—Oh, Haidee, I *did* want to see you married."

" Singleton, I beseech you don't break down —I shall scream or something awful—Kiss me —Oh, dear,—he's gone! Anne, come here—I cannot see at all."

She stood leaning against the kind old servant until the sound of the wheels died away in the distance. " Shall I ever see him again?" she muttered. " Anne, I'm so tired. I shall go to bed now. To-morrow—to-morrow—but I must not think now. Let me sleep while I can."

CHAPTER V.

WISHING to see the effect of the news of Singleton's departure upon her father and John, Haidee did not send his letter, but brought it down when she was ready for breakfast: for which meal she was exceedingly late. Reginald sprang up to meet her.

"I was quite frightened about you, particularly as you went off so early last night too. You are not ill, are you, Haidee?"

"Not at all, but I sat up very late—Singleton and I were so busy. And this morning I overslept myself. Papa, here is a note from Singleton. He has left home."

"Left home! provoking," muttered Sir Lionel. "Where—that is, do you know what he means to do?"

"He means to go abroad for a time," she answered vaguely. There was something in John's listening downcast face which made her determine not to mention Singleton's route. "He will go, I think, to Captain Hamilton, and remain perhaps, with him, but at all events abroad, until we hear of Black James."

She fancied that Sir Lionel, though surprised, was relieved; and she also fancied that John was very much put out: but she could not be sure. Reginald said nothing, but she saw that he was neither surprised nor sorry.

"I believe I am pleased," remarked Sir Lionel, after having read the note. "After the extraordinary conduct of Dr. Mostyn, I should have always been expecting to have this wretched boy upon my hands again. Doctors are such a very opiniated set of men. Perhaps, too, change of scene may benefit him: he never broke out into open violence while at sea, Reginald, did he?"

"Never more than a hasty temper would account for," Reginald answered. "Vernon indeed, and one or two others, once asked me if I believed him to be quite sane; but at the time I thought it only a careless expression."

"And what do you think it now?" Haidee asked: but he made no answer. After breakfast, he followed her as she was leaving the room.

"I must go home to-morrow, Haidee. Come

with me to the drawing-room. Don't run away from me this last day."

"Go to the drawing-room, and wait for me. I shall come to you soon, but I want to think quietly first."

"To think! of what?" She looked down at him (she was half way upstairs when he spoke) but she made no answer: merely saying, "I will come in less than an hour. Wait for me."

Reginald went to the drawing-room, and gave himself up to very uncomfortable reflections.

What could Haidee have to say to him that required so much thought? It must, of course, be something about Singleton. Now, Reginald was already sore and angry on that subject: he had (as Singleton said of him) a hundred good qualities, but undoubtedly, humility was not one of them: he was to the last degree proud and opiniated. Everything in his life, so far, had gone to foster his notion that he was always in the right: in fact, his conduct had always been so irreproachable that perhaps it was no wonder he should think so. As a boy he had been clever and industrious at school, pleasant and bright at home; while his elder brother had been idle and troublesome, and a tyrant among his sisters. Then they grew up, and the contrast was even more favourable to Reginald, as

Philip had been a heartbreak to his parents, while he was their pride and stay. Moreover, he had hitherto been so successful in life, that the idea of his will being resisted was new to him, and more new than acceptable. Even his love for Haidee had ministered to his pride —for while saying, as he often did, that he had been successful beyond his wildest hopes, he had a private conviction that he had not been successful beyond his merits. And now, to be told that he owed his success with Sir Lionel to Singleton— Singleton, to whom he had always accorded a kind of protecting affection! And it had been so pleasant to think that even Sir Lionel, whom others feared and disliked, could not resist his many perfections! Of course Reginald did not put these thoughts into words, but they existed, all the same, in that little dark cupboard we all keep a few thoughts in, in the back of our minds.

Also, he loved Haidee dearly and was very proud of her: but she was the first person who had ever differed from him in any serious matter, and she had maintained her opinion, even speaking sometimes as if she thought him to blame, as well as mistaken. This was a state of things quite foreign to his experience. It was a great pity that she had not been better taught: there was something almost unwomanly in these decided opinions, and her mode of expressing herself was too plain-spoken and unguarded. He did not doubt that she loved him; but she must learn to put him and his wishes first, and everything else (Singleton included) at a very respectful distance behind. His meditations brought him to the conclusion that it was his duty to speak seriously to Haidee: she would be angry at first, but he would be firm, and the sooner she understood him, the better for their future happiness. The idea that this happiness could be endangered by anything he might say to her, never entered his head. No—she would be vexed for a while, but would soon confess that he was right and sensible, she, wrong and absurd; they would be married as was arranged, on the fifth of next month, and when they were settled at Heronhurst, they would get Singleton to stay awhile with them, and see what could be done for him, poor fellow!

Having arrived at this point, he went into the conservatory to gather some flowers for Haidee. He had a mistaken idea that he could arrange flowers, and now spent some time in getting ready his offering, which looked very much as if he had accidentally sat down upon it when completed. He was still busy about it when Haidee came into the drawing-room. Her time too, had been passed in thinking, but oh! how differently. Her's had been no proud self-comfortings—her thoughts had been given to an earnest, humble endeavour to find out what her duty was, and to gain strength to do it. And now she thought she saw the right course to take, and she came to persuade him to agree to it, if possible—and in spite of Singleton's warnings, she still half hoped to convince him. Very lovely was the gentle tender look, which softened her bright beauty when she appeared before her lover.

"What are you doing in my dominions, Regie?"

"Getting what Hester used to call a 'real smell posy' when she was a child. See—a rose, some heliotrope, mignonette, and some of those sweet geranium leaves! isn't it sweet?"

"Very sweet," she said, smiling, as she put the flowers in her dress; "very sweet, Regie: all my favourites here, except violets; and I have none in bloom yet. Reginald! I want you to forgive me for my manner to you lately. I know I have been disagreeable—but indeed I have been so unhappy that I could *not* help being snappish. Say you forgive me, Regie?"

"Indeed I do, my darling," said Reginald warmly, disarmed by her sweetness and candour:

then a remembrance of his resolution made him add gravely, "I'm glad you have spoken first upon this subject, Haidee, for I want to say a few words to you—and what you have said will make it easier to both of us."

"Were you going to give me a lecture?" she said with a mischievous look; and yet there was much sadness in her voice and manner. "Well, I know I deserve it. Sit down here on the sofa beside me. Now, then, out with it, Regie; I am ready."

"My dear Haidee, you know I would not say a word that could hurt you."

"I do know it; but I really would rather you would speak plainly, if I have vexed you. You know, Reginald, you and I have to live our lives together; and there is nothing so comfortable as being frank."

"Well, you *have* vexed me, Haidee. You have expressed such very decided opinions lately—directly opposed to mine; and you have expressed them so strongly, and with so little regard for my opinion, which ought to have some weight with you; but as you are aware of it yourself, we need say no more about it."

"Ah, but I must, Reginald. Tell me, was it the fact that I differed from you, or my way of expressing myself, that vexed you?"

"Both, I think. I was sorry that my own dear girl could think me harsh and unkind."

"I am sorry," she said gently; "for I have told you that I know I spoke hotly and foolishly; but concerning Singleton, I think just the same still, and am still very, very sorry, and hurt too, that you should think as you do."

"There is no necessity for us to discuss the subject now, dear Haidee. Singleton has left England for a time; a very short time will prove whether his story is true, or—a delusion. No—I cannot deceive you—I must speak quite sincerely, and say that a very short time will open your eyes to the truth; and then you and I will get him to come to us, and see what will be most for his happiness. For I admit that Sir Lionel is mistaken in thinking that confinement——"

"Stop, stop, Regie. Sir Lionel has been wrong from beginning to end, and never yet was right in anything that concerned Singleton. Moreover, he is in this matter a mere tool in far more dangerous hands. But I don't want to argue the question with you; if your own heart does not tell you the truth, I must wait patiently until I can convince your head. But until that time comes——"

She paused, and he said quietly:

"If it is ever to be, it must be soon. Meantime, dear Haidee, though you are vexed because I differ from you, you cannot doubt that I shall help you loyally in defending him from any unnecessary suffering. Next month will give me a brother's right to help him, and a dearer right still to help you, and——"

"Regie! that's what I want to speak about. I have been thinking it all over, and I cannot help seeing that it will be better for us to—to put it off. Let us wait until his name is cleared. I cannot bear to think that he is away alone, miserable; and that I, his only sister, should take that time to be married."

"Haidee! I don't think I understand you!" he said in amazement. "Put off our marriage? Now, my dear girl, *do* be reasonable. How can you expect me to put it off, to wait for an event which I am firmly persuaded will never take place."

"But it *will* take place. Oh! why are you so hard, Reginald? I would risk my life on the certainty of his innocence, and I know we shall prove it one day. Mr. Seldon has undertaken to find out all about it."

"And yet you advised him on no account to risk a public inquiry, but on the contrary, to leave England as soon and as privately as he could! My dear, use your own good sense, of which you have plenty, and you'll soon see that Mr. Seldon's advice proves that he thinks as I do on this subject."

"I don't think so—he said he believed him; but tell me plainly, Reginald, what do you believe? I cannot understand exactly—tell me now."

"But if I attempt to tell you plainly, I shall only make you angry."

"No, I shall not be angry, indeed. Let me know distinctly what you think of my brother—what you really believe of him."

"I believe him to be quite incapable of anything cruel or ungenerous, when in his usual—his *best* state of mind and body; but I believe him to be one of those unhappy persons whose intellect is not as evenly balanced as is the general rule, and I think that his severe illness rendered this want of balance even greater than it had been before; so that when he got into those money difficulties, and in fact during all that happened, he was not accountable for his actions. I would not even undertake to say how far he himself believes the wild fiction by which he tries to account for it all; but between such a state of mind as this, and actual insanity, there is certainly a difference; and no one would be justified in keeping him in confinement for any length of time."

"I don't see that. If he is mad enough to invent that story, and then to believe it, he is mad enough for anything. Reginald, I *cannot* understand how you could live six years in constant intercourse with Singleton, and not feel sure of his sanity."

"Perhaps it is because I know him so intimately that I doubt it."

"Did you ever doubt it in all those years?"

"No. Others did, but I did not. My dear Haidee, I have never spoken to you frankly on this subject yet, partly from dread of hurting you, and partly because you have always silenced me when I have tried to approach it; but you really must listen to me now, for I cannot possibly allow such a monstrous proposal as you have made to pass in silence. It is quite time that you should understand me."

Rather irritated by a certain tone of authority in his voice, Haidee answered:

"I desire nothing so much as to understand you, my dear; but I'm afraid I shall find it difficult, however lucidly you may explain yourself. You lived for six years in habits of intimacy with Singleton, you came here with him and—became very intimate with me; you saw an attachment springing up between him and your own sister, and you seemed quite satisfied that it should be so. Now you imply that all this time you did not think him perfectly sane! I'm afraid it will take a good deal of the plain-speaking you promise me to make me understand this."

Reginald was silent, being too angry to trust himself to speak, and Haidee went on, after a pause : .

" You confess that you never suspected him of being mad until all this happened ?"

" I do confess it," he answered coldly. But I don't think that my confession proves much. Singleton is exceedingly fascinating — a most delightful companion ; and he attached himself to me in a way that would have won any one to love him in return. I know that my affection blinded me, but not completely ; for, as I think you know, I often spoke to him about his temper, which seldom showed itself when I was by, but was often strangely violent with others."

" But a violent temper does not prove a person mad, Reginald. At least, if so, half the people one meets ought to be in asylums. My father ought, certainly, and, indeed, myself, too ; for, as you have perhaps perceived lately, I have a touch of the same temper myself."

"I have perceived it, with very great pain; but there is this difference between you and Singleton. You *can* control it, and he can*not*."

"Oh, indeed, he can! I don't say he always does, you know, or did in those days that you are speaking of; but it was only because he did not try. No one ever taught him. I don't suppose it ever fitted into his head that it was wrong, until Hester took him in hand; and he was learning to control it. His manner to my father was as changed as possible, and he often bore a great deal in silence—ay, more than you would, Reginald!"

"Indeed!"

"Yes! I don't mind a hot word sometimes; but you cannot bear one not to agree with you in everything. You don't speak out, but you gloom and glower and look dignified, until— There! I am getting into a passion again, and I *did* mean to be so calm to-day."

"I cannot congratulate you on success. And as to your idea that Singleton was learning to control himself, we take very different views of that. I cannot see much self-control in his conduct of late; and I think that any one not wilfully blind must see that since his illness he has been decidedly odd. Why, when my father and mother were here he was so silent and low that you were unhappy about him, and then without any reason, he cheered up and became the life of the party. And that, remember, with those debts, and his confession to Sir Lionel, still hanging over him."

"I never said he was not variable in his moods; but that does not prove him mad, and I declare to you, that with Dr. Mostyn's plain statement that he is not and never was mad, I think very little of you as a friend that you choose to take the other side."

"Dr. Mostyn means mad enough to be kept under restraint. And as to your remark that you think very little of me because I cannot blind myself to the truth, take care, Haidee for I might say with much greater reason that I think very little of you because you choose to place your opinion in direct opposition to mine."

"Well!" said the girl excitedly, "if that means that you expect me to be always of your opinion in everything, I really cannot promise that, Reginald. I dare say there are women who can do that, but I am not one of them. I not only have my own opinions, but I claim my right to act upon them. And it is my opinion now, that you and I ought not to be married until we have come to a better understanding about Singleton.

For I know him to be speaking the truth, and shall act upon that belief; you believe John Trelawney in preference to either Singleton, Hester, or me; and altogether I think we ought to put off our marriage."

She suddenly turned to him with a pleading look in her eyes which made her for the moment wonderfully like Singleton.

"Will you wait one year, Regie? just one year. Surely it is worth while to wait that time for the hope of being married in happiness and real union, and not with this dreadful difference poisoning our lives."

It was a pity that she did not see how angry he was. But his way of being angry was so unlike anything she was used to, that she did not see it, and so took all he said at its fullest meaning, believing it said in cold blood.

"No, Haidee; I will not wait a year. Our wedding day is fixed—every one knows it: to put it off would cause endless talk and gossip, and make us all thoroughly ridiculous. No, I never will consent to it."

It sometimes happens that, when a flood of arguments rushes into our minds, we seize for use, in the hurry of the moment, upon the least effective. And Reginald had now used an argument which was not likely to weigh much with Haidee. He was really distracted at the idea of the happiness which had seemed so near being put off for so long a time, in order to wait for what he thought an impossible event. But he spoke only of what others would say, not of what he felt; and to his last words, "I never will consent to it," she answered quickly:

"You seem to forget that I can do it without your consent."

He started and turned to look at her.

"What do you mean?"

"I—I mean that it does not matter much whether people talk or not. Let them talk if they like, but I repeat, I think this is our only chance of happiness. We have done nothing lately but torment each other. Let us wait, Reginald, just one year. I will not ask more. This wretched business will surely be settled by that time, by the finding of James."

"It will never be settled; and in the meantime, think of the destruction this senseless delay would bring upon all our plans."

"How? I don't see."

"You know that the purchase of Heronhurst is to be completed as soon as we are married, and I cannot ask them to wait a year for their money."

Haidee reddened, as she looked at him in surprise.

6—2

"Your reasons are wonderfully unlike what I was prepared to hear," she said. "The world will talk—and you want money to pay for Heronhurst! If that is all, let the money be paid at once; I will get Sir Lionel to consent, it can make no difference to him, or to me."

"But a very great difference to me," Reginald said, his manner growing colder as he lost his temper more completely. "No, Haidee, that must not be. I should never feel sure whether you married me because you loved me, or because you felt bound by this transaction."

"Then let Heronhurst go! I love the dear old place, but it is not a matter of life and death, or of right and wrong. We can be happy elsewhere if we are to be happy at all—and we would be miserable there if this kind of thing were to go on—let Heronhurst go."

Colder and colder grew his manner, his voice, and the expression of his handsome face.

"You care little for my feelings in this matter," he said. "You forget that by your desire the offer for Heronhurst was made by me, in my own name; and that the day on which the money is to be paid is fixed; two days after that for our marriage. You forget in what a position you place me in the eyes of these people if I have to go and tell them that I am no longer in a position to keep my word."

Poor Haidee! in her bewildered state of anger and pain, it seemed to her as if the only reason he urged for refusing her request was that he wanted to buy Heronhurst, and to be able to pay for it. She spoke bitterly and angrily.

"You care more for buying Heronhurst than for my happiness. You seem to think of anything before that! But I am not going to do what I think wrong because you want to be master of Heronhurst—after all, as I said, I can put off my marriage if I like; and I *shall* put it off, whatever becomes of Heronhurst. I did not think you would put that first, Reginald."

The last sentence might have touched him; but it was said very low, and he was too angry to hear it, or to see the tears of mortification and pain that glittered in her eyes.

"You are mistaken in thinking that you can defer our marriage without my consent," he answered. "You can dismiss me, or marry me."

"But if I dismiss you, what's to become of Heronhurst?" she asked mischievously, a gleam of a smile passing over her face as she spoke.

"With that you have nothing to do," said

Reginald, thoroughly provoked by this last pin-prick. "If you do not marry me at the time fixed, I shall consider myself finally dismissed."

She started as if he had struck her.

"Dismissed!" she said breathlessly; "is that what you said, Reginald? All to be over between us for ever, unless I marry you at once?"

"I decline to postpone our marriage. Either dismiss me, or marry me."

"You are very arbitrary, and very cool about it, too. You spoke with more feeling about losing Heronhurst. May I inquire if it was only to become possessed of Heronhurst that you wanted to marry me?"

"You insult me," he said coldly; "but you would do better to consider what I say. Will you lay aside these ridiculous notions, promise to be guided by my judgment, and to become my wife at the time named; or will you put an end to our engagement, now and for ever?"

"I have told you that I cannot promise to be guided by your judgment, Reginald. I love my brother, however ridiculous that notion may appear to you, and I will not desert him. If you really mean that I must marry you next month, and never see him except as you permit and when you choose, or that you will never marry me at all—why you must do as you like:

only remember, it is your doing, not mine. I only ask you to wait."

"But to wait for what? a thing that will never happen. No—if you persist in this, you must dismiss me altogether. Is it to be so, Haidee? Are we to part?"

Haidee shivered as if cold, but her voice was steady, though sad.

"Are we to part? nay, we are parted. You are no longer *my* Reginald. I cannot help wondering if you ever *were* my Reginald, or if he was a dream of my own, and the hard, unfeeling, worldly man I have seen once or twice lately is the real Reginald. But—it is done and over now—so good-bye, Reginald, let us part in peace. I am—very sorry—and so are you, I suppose; but I was worth more than Heronhurst, if you could only see it. For I loved you—and believed in you."

"If your love and belief in me are destroyed, it is as well that we should part. I shall see Sir Lionel, and explain this to him."

"Very well. Go away now, please. I should like to be alone."

She buried her face in the sofa pillow, and did not look up again while he was in the room. When he left it, or how long she remained alone, she did not know, but at last a voice calling her by name roused her, and she started up, pale and wild-looking, in a half hope that it was Reginald come back to her. It was her father, however; and very much surprised he looked.

"Haidee, what does this mean? Reginald Hamilton has been to my room to tell me that you have dismissed him; declined to keep your engagement with him—is this so? or is it possible that *he* withdraws? I am aware that many men might object to marry into a family where insanity has appeared, but if he has withdrawn on that account, I shall feel it necessary to give him reason to regret that he has insulted my daughter."

"Oh no! I did it. I wanted to put off our marriage and he would not—I *cannot* marry him now. But it is my doing, papa."

Sir Lionel looked at her tear-stained face.

"You regret it now," he said more kindly than he often spoke; it touched even him to see this bright creature unhappy. "Shall I be your ambassador and hint to him that you have changed your mind?"

"No, papa," she answered slowly. "I have not changed my mind. What I have done, I must not undo; for I have done right."

He left her without urging her any more.

His mind had a marvellous amount of pertinacity about it, and all his hopes and schemes for marrying her to John revived in a moment.

Haidee went to her own room, where a violent headache kept her prisoner all the rest of the day; and before evening, Reginald Hamilton returned to London.

So ended the engagement which had begun so fairly.

CHAPTER VI.

HESTER HAMILTON was sitting by the drawing-room fire late on that same day, with a little writing-case upon her knee, and an open letter in her hand—Singleton's letter, which he had posted early in Plymouth; and which therefore reached Russell Square before Reginald's return. Mrs. Hamilton had not considered herself justified in suppressing it, and so Hester had it—and had it by heart now, so that nothing could rob her of it. Poor child, she had cried over it, and was crying still; and yet it had comforted her greatly, and she greatly needed comfort just then.

About half an hour ago, her mother had looked into the room, and said, "Your father is lying down, my dear, and I am going to read to him."

"Yes, mamma—but come in here for one moment first. I must tell you something."

Mrs. Hamilton shut the door, and prepared to listen, with rather an anxious look. Hester held out her precious letter. " I think you said you had read this, mamma ?"

" I did—it was sent to me open that I might read it."

" Of course. I want to answer it, mamma. Please think for a moment before you say no."

" Why should you answer it, Hester ? He does not ask for an answer."

" Poor Singleton! no, he does not. But I want to tell him that I believe him and shall always believe him, even if he never finds Black James. Of course, as you and papa will not allow it, we are not engaged, and I must write but this once; but I should like to write. You see, he is so sad—and every one against him : and I shall always feel just the same about him."

" My poor child, you are young, and don't know how time changes us. I should very much rather you did not write to him ; for even if you do not change, he may. It is better as it is, believe me. But don't look so unhappy, my little girl—I cannot bear to see my little Hester —who ought to be a child still, look thus. Hester," she continued hurriedly, " your father would be annoyed if you wrote to Singleton; but write to Haidee, and you may send a message—only remember, there must be no promise."

Having made this Jesuitical compromise, Mrs. Hamilton departed hastily; and Hester was writing her letter by the firelight when the door opened and in came Reginald.

"My dear Regie! how you startled me!" she exclaimed, hastily closing her blotting-book and putting her precious letter into her pocket. "We did not expect you until to-morrow."

"No—I said to-morrow when I wrote."

There was something about him which rather frightened Hester—and in order to see him better she stirred the fire to a blaze. He was pale, and looked very stern—she was afraid to ask him any questions.

"Papa is lying down, and mamma is reading to him. Shall I call her, Regie?"

"No—they will know all time enough. How is my father?"

"Very well, for him. He seems to gain strength every day."

"He will need all his strength. I have a bitter disappointment for him," said Reginald gloomily.

"I knew there was something wrong, Regie; what is it?" she asked timidly.

"What are you writing?" he said, turning a little away from her.

"I'm writing to Haidee. Have you any message?"

"None." He was silent for a few moments and then said, quietly enough, but with an evident effort: "You had better know the truth before you send your letter; but you must tell my father and mother—I cannot do it twice. Our engagement is at an end."

Hester started so violently that her writing case fell to the ground: then hurrying to his side, she put her hand gently upon his shoulder.

"Oh, Regie, this is dreadful! Why—how—did it happen? Oh, surely it will come right again!"

"No," he answered decidedly, "it never will. You may as well make up your minds to that. She spoke to me as no woman could speak to a man she really loved. It is all over between us—finally. Get my mother to break it to my father. I really dread the effect of his disappointment."

"Yes—he is so fond of Haidee; but indeed he will think more of you than of himself."

"He'll be terribly disappointed," Reginald said absently. "The idea of going back to Heronhurst has been new life to him."

"Oh, Regie, he will never give that a thought. It is your suffering that will grieve him."

"Nonsense, child: that is a girl's way of looking at it. My father was so pleased—so happy—and now——"

"I cannot understand Haidee at all! I must write to her."

"Not on this subject, I request you. Nothing that you or any one can say or do, will be of any avail. I wish it to be understood that nothing can be done, and that I prefer not to speak on the subject at all. I'm only sorry I cannot bear all the suffering and disappointment myself—but my poor father was so happy."

He left the room abruptly, leaving a very uncomfortable feeling in his sister's mind. His hard, constrained manner showed her that he was exceedingly angry, and she knew that his anger was no passing emotion. She laid aside the half-written letter which she had no heart to finish now, murmuring:

"Oh, if he should go on being angry until it is too late to make it up! I know he loves her! he will be so unhappy. I dare say she was very provoking."

Then she reluctantly sought out her mother to tell her the bad news, and Mr. Hamilton had to be told also. They were both greatly overcome, but Mr. Hamilton never thought of Heronhurst until Hester mentioned it.

"Heronhurst," he echoed half angrily; "who can think of that just now? My poor Haidee!"

"It was Reginald, papa. He feared that it would grieve you so much."

"So it will, no doubt, when I have time to think of it. Just now I can only think of all the sorrow and trouble that unhappy boy has occasioned—for of course it was about him they differed. It began before she went home."

Hester crept away, to cry quietly in her own room:

"Oh, Singleton! my poor Singleton! all laid down to you, who would give your very life to make them happy. It's not fair! Oh, it's not fair. But I will only cling the closer to him because others are unkind."

Next morning came a letter from Arthur Vane to his sister; written from Paris. He had met with a slight accident, and had sprained his ankle rather badly; Marian was staying at Versailles with some friends, so that he was alone and very helpless. If Reginald were not too busy preparing for the auspicious event of next month, it would be very kind of him to run over to his uncle for a few days, to be with him until Marian came back.

Mrs. Hamilton read this aloud, suppressing of course the "auspicious" allusion, and Reginald looked up from the book he was by way of reading, and said:

"I had better go to him."

"Indeed I think you will be the better for a little change," said his mother gently, looking sadly at his pale face.

"Yes—I shall be glad of a little variety. I think I shall go this afternoon."

"Oh, Regie," began Hester impulsively—and then stopped short, crimsoning all over.

"Well! what is it, Hester?"

"Nothing—never mind, Regie."

He looked at her in evident surprise, and so did her mother, but nothing more was said.

Reginald went to Paris, and his first letter announced that as soon as Marian had heard of her father's accident, she had returned to him. "So I am not wanted and shall be at home in a day or two," he added. But time passed and he did not come.

"Mamma," said Hester, when a fourth letter from Reginald gave no notice of return, "if you can spare me, I want so much to go for a few days to Haidee. She has never written to me since Reginald left her—and I want to be with her just now."

"My dear, I don't think you can go, your father would not like it," said Mrs. Hamilton thoughtfully. "I wish you could go, for I don't understand Haidee's conduct, and I am sure it only requires a little plain speaking to set matters right between her and Regie."

"Then let me go before it is too late, mamma. I cannot help feeling certain that Haidee never meant nor wished to break it off. In her last letter to me she said that she was beginning to see that it might be better to defer it for a time —until, perhaps, Black James is found. And my idea is that she proposed this and that he refused, and so they fought. But Regie *does* love her! a word from her would bring him back to her now, and, oh! I hate to think of the danger he is in."

"The danger! dear child, what do you mean? There is more than danger of his losing Haidee;—it is done."

"He is in danger of worse than that. Mamma, don't think me horrid for having such thoughts, and I will tell you what I fear."

"Tell me by all means, Hester; I have great faith in your clear-sightedness, and as you have rather frightened me, you may as well enlighten me now."

Hester put aside her work and pushed a low stool close to her mother. Then she sat down and laid her head on her mother's knees.

"Oh, mammie mine! what a thing it is to have a mother! If poor Haidee had a mother she would never have been saucy to Reginald; and if Marian had a mother she would never have been—what she is."

"My darling! I'm glad I am a comfort to you, for you have a heavy trial to bear. But Haidee's mother would not have been much comfort to her, I fear—she was a weak little creature. And what has Marian to say to it? You don't like Marian, Hester."

Hester made a most expressive little moue.

"No! I don't indeed. Now, mamma, I know you are a safe person, and so I am going to tell you a secret; and you are never to talk of it unless something happens which makes it necessary. I may be away then, so I mean to tell you. I am going to surprise you, you know."

"You are a perfect sphinx, my dear. What are you talking of?"

"Of my very pretty, soft-spoken cousin, Marian Vane. Now, mamma, I hate myself for seeing it, but I do see it. Regie has gone away, unhappy—bitter against Haidee, and trying to think that she never really loved him. More than that, he is dreadfully vexed about Heronhurst."

" Well ? that is not all, surely."

" That is only the beginning. Now Marian is in love—after *her* fashion, which is not mine, nor yours, mammie, with Reginald. This, I think, you probably saw for yourself."

" I suspected it, and told her of his engagement."

" I *knew* she had heard of it! and it made her ten times more set upon it than before; for Marian hates Haidee."

" Nonsense, darling! They hardly know each other. They met but once."

" Ah, but you know I was behind the scenes. Marian *hates* Haidee. If she can do it, she will marry Regie, simply to make Haidee wretched; and Regie did not care for her, but neither did he see through her. And she will let him see that she likes him, and be soft and yielding, and hint that if Haidee had cared much she would never have said this, and that; and she is rich, and he wants to buy Heronhurst."

" Hester! you surely don't suspect your brother of such a feeling as that! My dear, noble, good boy, who never gave us a moment's uneasiness in his life. I am astonished; I cannot think how such an idea got into your head."

Hester shook her head, as much as to say, "The idea is there, for all that."

"I was afraid you would be vexed with me, mamma; but it haunts me, and will not let me forget it. You don't know how he used to talk of Heronhurst, and of the happiness of seeing you and papa there again. And I saw that he was bitterly mortified at having to tell those lawyers that he could not buy it—has he told them yet, do you know?"

"No—he said he would write, or go when he came back."

"Well, mamma, I have told you my fear; but perhaps, after all, I only fear it because I have a bad mind. But now I am going to tell you facts. You wonder why I think Marian capable of anything heartless and wrong. When Singleton left Halifax he was engaged to her. He had always been in love with her, but she only played with him; and when he *would* speak, and she promised to marry him, she made him keep it secret until Sir Lionel had consented, for she said there was a quarrel between him and Uncle Arthur. Then, as you know, she became an heiress, and when next she saw Singleton she actually told him in plain words that she had never cared for him, and that when she accepted him it was only because she was so tired of Halifax and wanted to be married. That was just before his illness; but I don't think," added Hester, with a little toss of her head, " that he would have been ill about it, only that he kept on wet clothes all day and got a chill. She made him promise to keep it all secret; and when he was very ill, and I suppose she thought he would die, she wrote to Haidee to ask her to keep it secret too, whatever happened: and I think Haidee in her answer let her see what she thought of her. That is why she hates her."

"And Singleton was actually engaged to Marian! How very extraordinary—did my brother consent?"

"Yes, but not very willingly. Mamma, what was it all about? Sir Lionel was quite frantic with rage when his consent was asked, and Haidee really thought he would have killed Singleton. What happened that made all this dislike between him and Uncle Arthur?"

"I don't know why I should not tell you; it can do no harm; and as we are exchanging confidences, I think I shall. It happened when Sir Lionel first came to England. He was the heir, they found, after a great deal of litigation and trouble, and he came from America, where he had a great estate—in Virginia, I believe.

He went to stay with Mr. Trelawney, of Fair Forest, who would have been the heir but for this American cousin. And he passed there for an unmarried man. Mr. Trelawney had a beautiful sister; Sir Lionel fell madly in love with her, and proposed about a fortnight after he first saw her."

"And that was Marian's mother!" exclaimed Hester.

"Arthur, poor fellow, had been in love with her for a long time; but he was not in a position to marry. The day was fixed for the wedding, and it was quite near, when one day a lady walked into the solicitor's office where your uncle was learning his profession—a lady with a little boy—and that boy was poor Singleton."

"And she was his wife! Oh, mamma, what a horribly wicked thing! I would not have believed that of Sir Lionel."

"Well, of course it was very bad; but I know he proved that he had really doubted that his marriage was legal. Your uncle, having privately warned Mr. Trelawney, went to America, and quite satisfied himself and everybody that it was; but Sir Lionel appeared to have been under a false impression about it. Lady Trelawney was a Spanish Creole, and her grandmother had been a slave. I forget the exact story now, but Arthur was the active person in proving it all, and Sir Lionel was so enraged that Mr. Trelawney had to threaten him with public exposure if he molested Arthur in any way."

"And what became of poor Lady Trelawney?"

"She followed her husband to the Abbey, and I suppose he thought it better to acknowledge her and his son."

"But that is why he has never loved him; it explains everything that has puzzled us so much. I suppose I may tell Haidee?"

"It can do no harm that I know of, my dear?"

"And now, mamma, to go back to where we started—do contrive that I may go to Haidee. One word now may save them both from so much unhappiness; and I cannot write about it, because I don't know exactly what happened, and so I might do more harm than good."

"There is no hurry, Hester. Let her cool down a little and realise that she has lost him. I don't think that, under the circumstances, you can go uninvited; but I will speak to your father about it."

Mr. Hamilton, exceedingly fond of Haidee,

and terribly cast down by the whole affair, was far more propitious to Hester's wish than his wife, who dreaded that Singleton would come home. However the matter was settled in a day or two by a letter from Sir Lionel to Hester, urging her to come at once to the Abbey, as Haidee had shut herself up in her own room, and though declaring that she was not ill, would see nobody except her father. Sir Lionel entreated Hester to come and see if she could persuade her friend to be reasonable.

"For," said he, "although, as you are aware, I had other views for my daughter; yet I should infinitely prefer seeing her united to your brother, than that she should continue in the mental and bodily state in which you will find her,"

"Mamma, you will let me go now. Oh, my poor Haidee; but I wonder, when she is so sorry, why she does not write to me. I have never had a line from her, although I wrote to her."

"Since Reginald came home, or before?"

"Both—for I had begun my letter before he came, and I finished it afterwards."

"You never told me what you said—about that letter I mean. Did you send any message? I think I was very foolish to say you might."

"What harm could it do, mamma? for of

course I should tell Haidee, and she would tell him. It was only to me that it made any difference being allowed to send a message."

"And what did you say?"

"I said that I should keep his letter always, and that I believe and trust him altogether. And so I do, indeed. The only thing that surprises me is why Reginald does not feel as I do."

"My darling child, I hope your trust may be justified. Your father and I were talking of it only this morning, and I declare that but for Reginald's opinion—but after all Regie must know him!"

"Ah, mamma, don't you know that there are people who might live all their lives together and never understand each other? Regie does not know Singleton, though they spent six years together; and I do, though I knew him only for as many months. But we need not argue about it now. He and I must have patience— and we will. But I may go to Haidee, may I not?"

"Hester, you will never cease to think of him if you are to be there. It is sacrificing you to a chance of helping Haidee and Reginald."

"Mamma," said Hester steadily, "it will make no difference to me. I tell you plainly that I love him, and that when he asks me, I shall marry him, or I shall not marry at all. And you know that in your heart you don't believe in his guilt, and that when the time comes you will not forbid me. So you may as well let me go."

Mrs. Hamilton could not help laughing.

"You saucy child," she said. "Is this my modest Hester? Now if Haidee had spoken in this way I should not have been surprised."

"You see how much in earnest I am. But indeed, mamma, I did not mean to be saucy—please don't say that of me."

"No, my dear; but, oh, my little Hester, I wish you had never seen him."

"Ah, don't say that! even if I never see him again. Mamma, I am going to pack up. I suppose Dawson had better come with me, and come back next day."

CHAPTER VII.

HESTER was received with much pompous cordiality by Sir Lionel, who thanked her again and again for "so promptly acceding to his request," and who finally conducted her to Haidee's room himself. Throwing open the door he announced:

"I have brought you an unexpected, but I trust not an unwelcome visitor, Haidee."

Haidee raised her head slowly and reluctantly. She was lying on a low sofa, with her face turned away from the light.

"I am not ill, papa. I do not want to see Dr. Mostyn."

Hester looked at her in silent dismay. To see bright, beautiful, busy Haidee Trelawney lying thus alone, unoccupied, her brilliancy vanished, her eyes heavy with unshed tears—poor Hester felt as if the world were coming to an end. In all her sorrows she had been used to look to Haidee for comfort and strength, but Haidee seemed to want both now, and that sorely.

Sir Lionel merely replied:

"I think that you will find your guest a more welcome one than you seem to anticipate," and walked off, leaving Hester standing alone.

The sound of the closing door made Haidee look round, and in a moment more she had sprung from the sofa and thrown her arms round her friend, to whom she clung convulsively, her whole frame shivering with long-drawn sobs. Hester was frightened when she saw that neither words nor tears would come; nothing but those terrible gasps, and the pressure which told how lonely the poor child had been feeling.

"Haidee, dear, I'm so glad I came. Oh, my poor Haidee, how ill you look—how you have suffered! Why did you not send for me? Don't sob so dreadfully, dear; let me go—let me get you some water. Don't hold me so tight, dear; I can't move, and you are hurting me."

Then Haidee let her go, and sank down upon the sofa. She drank the water which Hester ran to bring her, and after some minutes was able to speak.

"Hester, it is well you came. I think I should have died—I have almost wished it."

"But you must not wish it, dear Haidee. That would be cowardly—like running away the first time there was really anything to fight against."

"A warlike idea, Hester; you, too, the gentlest of us all."

"The most cowardly, too, you should say; but perhaps that is why I always think of life as a battle; I am so afraid that I shall not fight bravely. But *you* are brave, Haidee — you won't give way."

"Ah, you are wrong there," Haidee answered sadly. "I *have* given way. I fought one great battle, Hester, and got wounded, I suppose; and ever since I have behaved like what you call yourself—a coward."

"You must be brave again now, then."

"I have never left this room since—that day. And poor papa has been really anxious; but I could not bear to meet John, who has worked all this misery, and would rejoice over it."

"But you must meet him some time, you know; and now we shall be together."

"Yes—but indeed, Hester, I think I have been very wrong not to try——"

"Don't blame yourself—you have been

stunned, I think. It was so dreadful and so sudden."

"Ah, no! not sudden," she answered dreamily. "For some time—even before I left London—I think I feared this. I saw that he thought I ought to agree with him in everything—and I could not. Yes—I think I expected it; and yet I know it has been partly my fault. I was not forbearing and gentle, as you would have been."

She looked so worn and weary that Hester, much as she longed to talk the matter over and try to act the part of peacemaker, felt that she must wait. She was trying to think of something to say when Anne came in, carrying a tray with tea and various tempting little dishes, which she set down on a small table and placed before Hester.

"You must want your tea, Miss Hamilton, after your journey," she said, as she arranged the tea things; then in a whisper—"coax her to eat, Miss Hester; she has touched nothing this day but a cup of coffee, and I cannot get her to hear reason."

Hester prepared two cups of tea and two plates of delicate bread and butter, with some lovely grapes; and then drawing Haidee to the table she said:

"Now this is my first order, and I am going to be a very strict mistress, you naughty girl. Drink this cup of tea—every drop of it—I will give you some more then. Now—you are not to leave one bit of this bread, no, nor one solitary grape. You look like a ghost, and no wonder, starving yourself in this foolish way."

"But I did not feel starving, I could not eat. O you wretched Anne, you've been informing against me."

"Indeed yes, ma'am, and it was about time that some one should know that you were killing yourself, and take care of you! and I knew Miss Hamilton would manage you, though I could not."

Haidee began to eat to please Hester, but she continued the operation to please herself.

"I declare I believe I was hungry without knowing it, Anne. I am leaving no bread and butter for Miss Hester."

"I have more here, ma'am," said Anne, producing another plate. "You really look less ill already."

"Well, I did really try yesterday, Anne! and I could not swallow. Now, take the tray away, we have had enough."

"Now, Miss Hester, make her go with you and walk up and down the south passage, while I open these windows and give the room a good airing. Here's a shawl for you, ma'am."

"But," said Haidee reluctantly, "you will be tired, Hester."

"I shall be glad to walk about a little, the railway tires me so. I suppose we could not go out?"

"Oh no! I think it is too—cold—or dark, or something. No, I will go to the passage, but that will do for to-day. Poor Anne! she has been unwearying in her attempts to get me to do this and that and eat every half hour, but I really could not, although I knew I ought."

"You were alone—now it will be different when I am with you."

"Different indeed! I think you brought life back with you, Hester."

The two girls wrapped up in the same shawl (an old habit of theirs), paced slowly up and down the dim corridor—a very good place for a confidential talk.

"Haidee, I did not think you were one to give way so much."

"Did you not? Neither did I, for that matter. But—it all came at once, and I had no one to say a word to."

"But you were always the brave one among us, to whom I looked for help and strength."

"Ah, Hester! but those sorrows were not like these. It was dreadful for mamma and Mr. Hamilton, but *we* had our lives before us, and nothing could make things so sad; even leaving —Heronhurst."

The word came out with a little sob; and Hester noticed it.

"Yet there are bright days in store for us still, dear Haidee. This will pass away, if you will be wise."

"I shall try to be wise; but my wisdom now must be submission, and it is a hard lesson to learn. Hester, you and I have no secrets between us—and I am going to tell you why I am so very unhappy. O Hester, it is not only that I have lost him—but I am disappointed in him. *Don't* be angry! it is such a comfort to tell you all."

"I am not angry. I have no right to be, for I share the feeling myself, a little."

"Do you? and why? For my part, I know I was angry, and perhaps exaggerated in my own mind what passed; but I declare to you it seemed as if he thought more of losing Heronhurst than of parting with me. And then he was so hard! so cruelly hard about Singleton."

"He is—I confess that. But as for Heronhurst, I believe he was thinking of poor papa, who was so happy about your engagement, and Reginald thought that it was all about Heronhurst—while all the time it was simply because he is so fond of you. You must remember that Regie having been so long away, does not know how fond papa is of you, and so made this mistake."

"You're a good special pleader, Hester. Where is he now?"

"In Paris with Uncle Arthur and Marian."

Hester glanced at her companion to see if she looked annoyed, but the beautiful pale face did not change.

"Haidee, dear, you will—you surely must, forgive poor Regie. I know you have reason for your anger, but no one is quite perfect, and when we love a person we ought to love him in spite of his faults, don't you think?"

"But I don't know that I am angry—and I am not unforgiving, Hester, only—disappointed. And it does not matter much what I feel, except to myself."

"But though you are disappointed, you love him still, even with his faults?"

"And what of that?"

"If he knew it, it would make a great difference to him, Haidee. He is very unhappy. And I get quite frightened about him sometimes, because he is not one to bear sorrow patiently. He will rebel—try to throw it off—and I am always expecting to hear that he has done something rash—and wrong."

Haidee was roused now, and looked anxious enough.

" If any one else said this to me, Hester, I should think it was only to influence me: but you don't speak unless you believe what you say. And you are so dreadfully keen-sighted. What do you fear for him—tell me?"

" Haidee, I hate myself for the thought—but I will confess it to you. He has gone away, bitter and angry as well as unhappy. Uncle Arthur sent for him, and Marian was away; but she came back, and is there now. And oh, Haidee, she is a dangerous girl, because she will stop at nothing to gain her ends, and she loves him after her fashion of loving—and she hates you. And remember she is rich: and there is Heronhurst still to be bought. Oh, it is a great temptation."

Haidee let go her companion's arm, threw off her share of the shawl which covered them both, and walking quickly on, she stood by a window looking out into the gathering darkness, her chest heaving, her hands clasped together. Hester waited, half frightened. Presently, in a low voice, Haidee said :

"You really think this, Hester? You believe it possible that Reginald may marry Marian Vane, in order to purchase back Heronhurst?"

"Remember, he knows no harm of her. I thought Singleton would forgive me, and I told mamma, that she might warn Reginald if she saw cause for fear."

"You told mamma—and what did she say?"

"She was nearly angry with me for thinking such a thing possible."

"And so should I be, if——"

She broke off suddenly and said no more.

"You'll be so cold, Haidee : come under the shawl again."

Haidee complied, and they took a turn or two in silence. Then she said :

"Come back to my room now—I am—oh, so tired."

"But you will dress and come down to dinner, won't you? Do, dear Haidee! you will really be ill if you shut yourself up so."

"I will come. John left the Abbey to-day, so I do not care so much."

They sat down by the fire, and for some time

not a word was said. At last, Haidee said very quietly :

"What did you think I could do, when you told me this?"

"Are you angry with me, Haidee?" cried poor little Hester, her eyes filling with tears; for the face she knew so well looked almost stern in its new gravity.

"O no, a thousand times no! My little Hester—I've actually made you cry. Don't, my darling, or I shall feel like a beast. I am not angry, only—stunned, I think. But tell me what you want me to do."

"I want you to let me tell him that you love him still."

"He knows it without telling."

"Yet—let me write. There is time even this evening—O Haidee, let me write."

"Not this evening. I don't think I can do it—but I will think. I will tell you sometime, soon."

"Oh, don't delay. If there is any danger, it is *now*. If he had time to think, he would be in no danger."

"To-morrow I will tell you then."

"And now, Haidee—it is getting late, you know—so please tell me, have you heard from Singleton?"

"You patient little thing—I ought to have remembered that you have not heard. Yes, he has written very often, and his are the only letters I have opened except yours. He is well—and on his way to Captain Hamilton. I have been shamefully selfish, Hester. I have never written to him—and your message will comfort him so much. But then, I know he will be so vexed about me, because he implored me not to quarrel with Reginald on his account."

"Yet you could not give him up—he will know that. Why, here is Anne! you don't mean to say that the dressing-bell has rung, Anne?"

"It has, ma'am: some time ago, too. Why, Miss Trelawney, you look more like yourself already."

Hester privately wondered what poor Haidee had looked like before—for she almost thought she might have passed her without knowing her. The two girls dressed in haste and went down together. Sir Lionel seemed really pleased to see his daughter, though even he, dull and unobservant as he was, felt shocked at the change those few days had wrought in her.

At dinner, he took occasion to announce the unwelcome news that John had gone to town to complete his arrangements for selling out, and that henceforth he would reside altogether at the Abbey. Haidee looked up quickly, but a glance from Hester reminded her of the presence of the servants, and she checked herself until they had left the room. Then she said :

"Papa, I am very sorry that John Trelawney is to live here, for I dislike and distrust him—more than distrust him, as you know. But you are the master here of course, and can have him if you like; only it is fairer to say at once that I shall never exchange a word with him when I can help it, and that I wish him anywhere else."

"I have not now to learn the fact of your silly and unfounded suspicions, Haidee. But I desire that you will behave to my guest as the mistress of my house should behave ; and I trust to time to open your eyes to your own absurdity."

No more was said upon the subject, and the two girls soon left the room.

Next day Haidee came down to breakfast, and resumed her usual employments, but it was evidently an exertion to her, and she looked wan and weary. It was a dull, wild day, not pleasant enough to tempt them to go far, but after luncheon the two girls went on the terrace to get a little fresh air. Here, as they walked up and down, Haidee said:

"I promised to tell you what I think of your wish to write about me, Hester. You startled me very much by your fears for him—you thought I was angry with you, but I was much nearer being angry with myself for *not* being angry. If I still trusted him as completely as I *must* trust him, if I am to love him, I should simply have laughed your suspicions to scorn—and I would give the world to feel that."

"Yet you will not, because you cannot, quite cease to love him because he is not quite as perfect as you once thought him."

"You are right; but between quite ceasing to love him, and what I did feel, and do not feel now—and shall never feel again—there is a long, long way, Hester. I cannot send him any message—not even to stop him marrying Marian Vane, if he really would do it. Put yourself in my place, and you will see that I am right. I should be very miserable, because having once believed—no, I don't believe it—but doubted that he might be guilty of such a meanness, how should I ever be sure that he was not?"

"Do you mean that if he were capable of

being tempted to do it, you would not marry him?"

"I think I should not. And this I know, that if I did we should both be miserable. I always doubting, and more than half despising, he knowing that it was so."

"And yet, Haidee, if this happens, you will be wretched."

"I shall—I dare not think of it, for fear I should be weak enough to do as you would have me. Believe me, Hester, I am right. I cannot say a word now, but when he comes home I will write to him."

"And what will you say?"

"What should I say but 'come back, Regie,' the girl said softly; 'come back, if you can forgive and forget.' But this is, if he comes back from Paris untempted—at least, unfallen. If he could do that, I never could get over it."

"O Haidee, have you thought of what you are risking? You cannot conceal from me that you love him and dread losing him. Why not give him the one word of hope that might save him?"

"Because the plain truth is, that he knows how I feel perfectly well. He knows that I love him, and never had the smallest intention of sending him away. However angry he may be, he knows all this; and if he marries her, it is not because he doubts *my* love, but because his love was more set on Heronhurst than on me. And in that case he is not the Reginald whom I love, but the Reginald of whom I have unwillingly caught a glimpse now and then lately. And if I knew that my sorrow would last through a long life—for to die at once would be nothing to that!—even then I would take up my burden and try to bear it."

"Then I have no more to say. If you feel thus, you are right. I can only pray for him that he may resist the temptation, for tempted I know he will be."

"Any man may be tempted; but if this would be a great temptation to him, let him go. If a look would bring him back to me, I would not look. And now let us say no more about it. By the way, what did mamma say when you told her about Marian and Singleton? I was wondering last night as I lay awake."

"She was very much surprised. But do you know, she told me the reason of Sir Lionel's dislike to poor Uncle Arthur; and I said I should tell you."

"Of course you will! and quickly, too; for on this subject my curiosity won't bear trifling with. Was it anything about my mother, Hester?"

In reply, Hester told the story just as it had been told to her.

"But what on earth made him fancy that the marriage was not legal?"

"I don't know. I forgot to ask."

"My mother was a Roman Catholic, I know; it may have been something about that; they were married by a priest very likely. One thing I am very sure of—*she* never doubted that she was his wife. No one could look at her face and believe that she was anything but a pure, innocent child. Have you ever seen the picture of her that Singleton has?"

"Yes, he showed it to me."

"So she really had black blood in her veins? there was that much truth at least in John's sneers."

"Very little, though."

"Oh, I don't care," Haidee answered indifferently. "It does not show, for though Singie is dark, it is a Spanish-looking darkness. I really don't see that it is of any consequence; but I can see, now that I know it, that my father does not agree with me."

"Let us go in now, Haidee. It is cold, and besides I want to write to mamma."

"Very well. I think I will put in a line too. I must beg her not to shut me out of her heart, even if—things go wrong."

"She does not blame you much; indeed, just at present all the blame gets laid upon poor Singleton, who was only trying to secure your happiness. Ah, Haidee! I hope we may be able to make it up to him one of these days."

"I hope so, poor old fellow! he has had a troubled life so far, but I cannot altogether pity the man who has your love, Hester—and deserves it," she added bitterly. "Come, let us go in."

CHAPTER VIII.

TIME passed, and Reginald did not return to London. He wrote pretty frequently to his mother, and his letters were affectionate and interesting; yet there was something wanting, something changed, which the mother's heart felt, though she could not say exactly what it was; and, indeed, persuaded herself that the tone which startled her was due to grief at the breaking off of his engagement with Haidee. Yet, though she told herself that she believed this, she would have given worlds to be able to forget Hester's strange warning. She wrote to him, begging him to come home; but he took no notice of the request. Then she wrote to tell him whither Hester had gone, and that she found Haidee far from well; he still took no notice. Then she inquired about Marian; was she improved? did he like her better than of old? and owned that she herself had not been much attracted by her. To this he replied that Marian's beauty had not, he thought, increased, but that she was very pretty; but that her manners had so much improved since she had mixed more in society, that she was hardly the same being. "Her attention to Uncle Arthur, too, is wonderful, in one so much admired and sought after. She would never leave him but that he insists on it sometimes. I really think she only requires a steady hand over her to make her all that a woman ought to be, for she is gentle, yielding, and docile, a very refreshing contrast to the type of young lady in fashion at present. Her faults are in great measure owing to her father's indulgence, and, indeed, poor Uncle Arthur has always been very weak, and now that his health is failing he is weaker than ever."

This letter gave Mrs. Hamilton a sleepless night, and the next day she wrote again to her son, taking two hours to get through her task, though it was not a very long letter when completed. But it was so difficult to say enough and not too much; she wanted to say that she knew Marian to be an unprincipled flirt, while she did not feel justified in telling the story of her behaviour to Singleton plainly. So she merely hinted at it, saying enough, she thought, to make Reginald pause and ask for an explanation, if he had any such thoughts as she feared.

The fifth of January was the day which had been fixed for the marriage of Reginald and Haidee, and the purchase of Heronhurst was not to have been concluded until after the wedding. On the seventh, Mr. and Mrs. Hamilton were surprised by the sudden appearance of Reginald, who arrived while they were at dinner.

"He has come to ask me what I mean," thought his mother, "and I shall be able to save him, even if that artful girl has been tempting him."

But dinner must be disposed of and the servant got rid of, before they could have any private conversation. Reginald said he was hungry, but she noticed that he could not eat, and that every now and then he forgot what he was doing and fell into deep thought; not pleasant thought, if one might judge by his face. When dinner was over, and they were seated in the home-like drawing-room, Mr. Hamilton half dozing by the fire, she began by inquiring how her brother was when Reginald left him.

" Better," he answered absently.

" But I fear from your account that he does not really improve. I had no idea until you wrote about him that he was such a confirmed invalid."

"Well, he is very much broken. He looks older now than my father, and he is younger, isn't he?"

"Ten years younger: poor Arthur! And Marian—how is she?"

"Very well—perfectly well, thank you," he answered hurriedly.

His manner became less like himself every moment, and his face wore an expression, half defiant, half anxious, which was quite new to it. The calm confidence which once characterised him had given place to an uneasy mixture of doubt and triumph: his mother could not understand him at all. She glanced at her husband, who was now nearly asleep, and said in a low voice:

"Did my letter surprise you, Regie?"

"Yes," he said, recovering his composure by a very visible effort; "it did: and I asked Marian for an explanation. You were alluding, I think, to what passed about her and Singleton Trelawney?"

"I was: did she tell you the whole story? It is not likely that she did, and as I have no further motive for silence I shall tell you all I know."

"Quite unnecessary. I know all I care to know. She was engaged to him, and broke it off when Sir Lionel refused his consent. She never cared for him, but she was very young and easily persuaded—easily frightened too, and he half frightened her into it. She was glad of an excuse to end it—in fact, before they met again she had opened her eyes to the fact that she not only did not care for him, but that she preferred—some one else."

"But, Regie, let me tell you——"

"Stay, mother—forgive me if I say I would rather not hear you. It can make no difference now—and I know the truth better than you can. I cannot wonder enough at the fact that you have ever heard of it. It is a thing which an honourable man would never have mentioned."

"It was Hester who told me, and she did so only that I might warn you if I saw you in danger."

"And Hester heard it from him, of course. I don't wish to hear another word on the subject. The affair concerns no one so nearly now as it concerns myself, and I am satisfied that Marian was not to blame. She was foolish to promise, but if his father had consented she would have kept her word, and as it was she had a valid excuse for freeing herself. Fortunately—for she was afraid of him, and her account of his violence justifies her fear. She has no doubt that he is insane."

"Did you hear all this from her, or from her father?"

"From her, but he confirmed her story, as far as facts go. He was very much vexed at the whole affair, and dislikes talking of it."

Then he turned to his mother and said:

"Are you convinced that Marian was not much to blame, mother?"

"You have not heard the other side. No, Regie, I am not convinced."

"You never liked her from the first, she says."

"She is right. I never quite trusted her— her words never seemed to me to represent her real meaning, or thoughts rather."

Reginald stood up and began to poke the fire, which by no means wanted poking. His father woke up at the sound.

"You'll roast me, my boy. Pull my chair a little back—thank you. By the way, Regie, you ought to let —— and Sons know that you —are not going to purchase Heronhurst."

"I went to the office on my way here."

Mr. Hamilton sighed slightly. Reginald bent over him and took his hand gently.

"My dear, dear father! one consolation I have—whether I have done well for my own happiness or not, I hope I have secured yours. Father—mother," he went on, drawing himself up to his full height and speaking very slowly, "I married my cousin, Marian Vane, yesterday morning, with her father's full consent. And by his desire I paid the full sum agreed upon for Heronhurst to-day; and the old place is ours."

There was a dead silence of many moments: then Mrs. Hamilton burst into tears, while on her husband's kind face a cloud gathered, the first Reginald had ever seen there when his father looked on him.

"Reginald—say that again? I think I must be dreaming. Married! did you say you were married to Marian Vane?"

"I did, father. I don't wonder that you are surprised, but I am sure you will forgive me for not having waited for your formal consent. I had quite made up my mind that Marian would —make me happy—happier than I deserve to be. And she wished it—the fact is, that she has long liked me, and when my mother's letter showed that there was a prejudice against her here, she declared that if I left her I should never return. And Uncle Arthur thought it would be better to pay for Heronhurst at once and have no explanations."

"A prejudice!" exclaimed Mr. Hamilton, "who has a prejudice against her? I merely thought her a pretty, silly little thing, not to be named in the same day with—but that's no matter. There may be no great harm in the girl, though she must have been in a desperate hurry to be married, that she could not wait until you even announced it to your own father. But there's a great want of womanly delicacy in lending herself to help you in putting such an insult upon Haidee Trelawney."

"No insult, sir! she had dismissed me."

"No insult! Good Heavens, that I should live to hear a son of mine say such a thing! No insult—to prove to her so that a fool must see it, that what you wanted was a wife with money —money to buy Heronhurst; and that, *that* secured, Haidee or Marian—the name mattered little."

"Henry! don't be so severe," pleaded his wife.

"Nay, mother, I suppose you think the same. Let my father say all he feels. I thought I was making him happy, at all events."

"Happy! I tell you, when I left Heronhurst, I said that disgrace should never sit beside my father's hearth—and when I looked forward to ending my days there with you and my darling Haidee, I thought you loved and valued her as she deserves. I thought you were worthy of her. I never put her money first. But now, Reginald, I will never enter Heronhurst. The worst disgrace, the disgrace of a mean and sordid spirit, buying and selling instead of loving and marrying, will be there—I shall see the old place no more. Hester—my poor old woman! come here. Don't sob so pitifully, my darling."

She came and knelt beside him, and laying her head upon his shoulder, sobbed out:

"Oh, Henry, our sons! our two beautiful boys that we were proud of!"

Reginald covered his face with his hands and groaned. That his mother should name him and his unhappy lost brother in the same breath! She could say nothing half so bitter as that; and leaving his parents in their sorrow, he stole from the room.

They saw him no more that night, and next morning he left the house before his mother came downstairs. She had a terrible task before her. Hester must be written to, Haidee must be told the truth, before she saw it in the papers. At about one o'clock Reginald came back, and found her in the drawing-room, writing; and just as he entered she laid down her pen and wept bitterly. Oh, it was hard to write that letter! To confess that her darling and pride, her stay and support, had so terribly disappointed her; to blight poor Haidee's young life; to grieve Hester, who had griefs of her own already, it was not wonderful that the hot, painful tears, wrung from eyes no longer young enough to weep easily, fell one by one upon the paper, blotting and blurring the writing so that it was scarcely legible. But she heard him move, and hurriedly drying her eyes, she began to fold and address her letter. He bid her good-morning, and then, standing by the fire, asked:

"Where is my father?"

"He is not up yet. He had such a bad night."

"Then I will not disturb him, I have finished the business I came over about, and shall return to Paris at once. The tidal train starts at two."

"You will want some luncheon," she said, half rising.

"No, it is too early. I can get some at Dover."

"And when do you return to England, Reginald?"

"In about a month. We think of making a little tour while my uncle stays at Wiesbaden for a while. Then he will come home with us.'

"Then we shall see you in a month," she answered.

"That depends altogether upon yourselves. If we shall be welcome, we shall come. If not, you need only be silent and we shall not trouble you."

"I do not understand you, Regie."

"Why, from what my father said last night, I cannot count upon his receiving my wife as— as I should like her to be received. My father spoke very plainly of what he considers her faults; now whatever faults she is guilty of, I certainly led her into them, or was the cause of them. So I am the more bound to see that she does not suffer for them."

"It would be a great change in your father, Reginald, if he failed in courtesy to any woman."

"I know he would be courteous, and so would you, mother. But there are many kinds of courtesy: and I may as well say plainly that having married Marian, I mean to do my duty by her. So if we are invited, we will come; and if you don't want us, don't invite us. There's no more to be said, I think."

"No more, Reginald? No message for your father?"

"Except that I beg him to think again about coming to Heronhurst. Now, mother, don't use your influence against me."

"I will not. But your father will hold to what he said, Reginald. He has the keenest sense of honour; nothing will change him in this."

Reginald coloured high, and said stiffly:

"I cannot see, even yet—in what my dishonour lies. But we need not argue—what I have done, is done—and I am content. And now I must be off, mother."

He crossed the room, and bent to kiss her; as he did so his eye fell on the address of her letter to Hester. He was pale already, but now for a moment his face was ghastly, and he stared blankly at the familiar address as if it were reproaching him aloud—for a moment she thought he must break down altogether. But his master passion, pride, was strong within him. He recovered himself, bid her farewell and left her. She was still sitting by the writing-table when a servant brought her a letter.

"Mr. Reginald bid me give you this, ma'am, and say it was in his greatcoat pocket, and he forgot it until now."

She opened it with a sigh.

"From Arthur. O poor Arthur! in your weakness you have contrived to ruin my boy."

"My dear Hester,

"Reginald will have told you all that there is to be told by this time. I hope you and Hamilton will not be annoyed at our hasty proceedings. I wanted them to wait for your consent, but they preferred being married first and getting your consent afterwards, and I did not object as I should have done unless I felt quite certain that you would both be pleased. Marian has told me how little you liked the intended marriage with that beautiful, ill-tempered Miss Trelawney, who seems to have acted just as her father's daughter was sure to act. My dear girl has loved Reginald ever since she was old enough to know her own mind, and it gives me more satisfaction than I can express to place her in such safe hands. She needs only the guiding hand of such a man as Regie, to be to her husband all that my dear Marian was to me. It seemed a pity to have any trouble or delay about Heronhurst when the matter could be so easily arranged. I have enabled Reginald to pay at once, and shall make them a suitable allowance while I live, and at my death all will go to them of course. I trust we shall see many happy days at Heronhurst, all of us; and although Reginald has of course never opened his lips about that affair, yet from what Marian tells me I think he knows that he has had an escape. Imagine being tied for life to Sir Lionel in petticoats."

The letter went on to give details of their plans, etc. Mrs. Hamilton did not know whether she was more inclined to laugh or to cry.

"Poor dear Arthur," she said to herself, "how completely that girl has hoodwinked you. What an artful creature! what a tissue of lies and artifices she must have concocted, to blind them both so thoroughly. Well! as he says, it is done, and the only thing to hope for him now is that he may never find her out; but he is not poor Arthur; I fear he will see through her only too soon. My sweet loving Haidee—Sir Lionel in petticoats." She drew her writing-book towards her—then pushed it away. "I will leave him in his delusion—what does it matter? The child's heart will be nearly broken—what will she care what Arthur thinks of her?"

And she never answered the letter at all.

The same post which took Mrs. Hamilton's letter to Trelawney Abbey, brought to Haidee a line from Marian Vane—or rather from Marian Hamilton. It was short, and contained the following words :

"I have delayed my thanks for this letter longer than was perhaps courteous. But I think you will acknowledge that I owe you nothing now.
"MARIAN HAMILTON."

Enclosed was her own plain-spoken letter to Marian, written during Singleton's illness.

CHAPTER IX.

FOUR years have passed away. In the tender dusk of a soft spring evening Haidee Trelawney is walking slowly up and down the terrace at the back of the Abbey. She is dressed in deep mourning, and her face, once so bright, is sad enough to go well with her dress. And yet there is something that is not sadness, too; there is expectation, and hope, and the sweet face has lost nothing in beauty, though much that made the beauty of its spring is gone for ever. She looked at her watch.

"He will be here in half an hour now. 'Late, late in the gloamin' Kilmeny came home.' Oh, my dear Singie, how I do long for you! How heartsick and lonely I am till you come!"

A soft voice behind her replied:

"My poor Haidee! I will never leave you again, my dear."

She sprang away in the first surprise, then

turned, and flying back clasped him in her arms. No word could she say, but the clinging embrace was eloquent enough. He kissed her cheek, her brow, her lips, murmuring tenderly:

"My Haidee — poor darling — lonely and heartsick!—my bright beauty—sad and sorrowful! But I must try to be all to you, Haidee. We love each other, don't we, darling? and at least we shall be together now."

"Singleton! let me hold you—it does me good to feel you — to squeeze you tight — to know that I have you safe."

"To part no more, Haidee."

"You—did you get my letter, Singleton?"

"No, I got no letter—a telegram which found us at Malta, and I came home as fast as I could. But I know all, dear—the servants 'Sir Singletoned' me at once."

"Come in and let me see you, Singie; I have only felt you as yet."

She drew him through Sir Lionel's porch, and on into the drawing-room, which was a blaze of light (Haidee loved a well-lighted room). And there was a fire, too, lest the traveller should be cold. She turned and took his cap from his head, that she might see him the better, and he looked at her in return. Her eyes filled with tears and her lip trembled.

"What is it, Haidee?"

"Is this you, Singie?—where's my boy brother, with the bright eyes and the saucy smile?"

"Gone, dear. You've a man in his place, and I think a better man than the boy promised you, though that is not saying much for him."

"Am I as much changed as you are, Singie?"

"You are lovelier than ever!" he exclaimed warmly. "Changed — yes, you are, I think. There's a softer, quieter look, and a little less colour; but you are the loveliest thing I have seen since I saw you last, my darling."

"I'm glad you think so, because it shows that you love me, Singie. Otherwise it does not much matter, does it? Now I must ring and get you some dinner; I dare say you are famished, and I quite forgot it."

"I am not hungry, but we had better get dinner over, for I have so much to tell, and more to hear."

She rang the bell, and Pierce came in.

"You may send up dinner as soon as possible, Pierce."

The man looked at his young master, answering mechanically:

"Yes, ma'am." Then he made his way to Singleton's side. "Mr. Trelawney—Sir Singleton, I mean to say—*can* you forgive me, sir ? I know now what an ass I was, and if you'll believe me, sir, I could lay 'ands on myself with pleasure when I think how I let those two pernicious villians make a tool of me—thinking myself so sharp, too. If you tell me you can't abear the sight of me, and that you must have a new butler, it's no more than I deserve ; but if you can overlook it, you'll have a faithful servant, Sir Singleton."

"What has changed your mind so much, Pierce ?"

"Miss Trelawney knows, sir ; but, indeed, that was only the end of it, like. We had all come round to see the truth, sir."

"Well, Pierce, I like to see old faces around me ; and so I'm glad you've found out your mistake—it was only a mistake as far as you were concerned, I know. Shake hands, and say no more about it. Tell the rest it's all right ; there was no one to blame except——"

"Except them pernicious villians!" interrupted Pierce, who evidently considered the phrase a telling one. "Thank you, sir ; you've taken a load off my mind," he added, as he left the room.

Singleton smiled.

"Poor old Pierce ! But Haidee, where are

the two pernicious villians—or rather where is John?"

"I believe he is in Plymouth. He remained here until the funeral, and then he wanted to have the will read; but I would not consent to that, and Mr. Seldon helped me. He wanted to stay here till you came, but I would not have that either. Mr. Seldon is to be here to-morrow, and then John will come too."

"Was it not unusual to want to read the will without the presence of the next heir?"

"Quite unusual; but let us have some dinner, my dear, and then I will tell you all that you want to know."

Dinner was soon disposed of. Poor Sir Lionel, he would have been shocked at the hurried proceedings; and the brother and sister returned to the drawing-room.

"Now, you tired-looking mortal! you shall sit here in this great chair—and I will sit here where I can look at you and feel sure you are really there—and we must have a great talk."

"Yes; I must ask you to tell me what has happened. I know only what your telegram said: 'Sir Lionel very ill and asks for you.' I hurried home; but the servants told me I was too late. Did my father really ask for me?"

"It was almost the only thing he said. Oh,

Singleton, it was a terrible — an awful scene. He could not speak distinctly, and all one side was paralysed."

"But he was so young for that! and such a strong, healthy man."

"Phillips says now that he had had many threatenings, and I know he had been to town about his health. But you know how it was—when he found that I positively would not marry John, nor believe all that story about you, he quite lost all affection for me. Sometimes days would pass without my seeing him. John was always with him. Oh, it has been a dreary time."

"Enough to drive you mad. But tell me about his illness."

"I was in the library writing to you. Papa went out and spoke to the gardener's men who were filling the flower-beds—he was not pleased and spoke loud and swore a good deal at them. Then he went away towards the oak wood. I had seen John go that way before; but he was alone then, and they tell me that Phillips was with him when they came back."

"Came back with my father! Haidee, was there foul play?"

"No, O no: there was no sign of violence. Papa came back alone. I heard a strange shouting, and fancied it was some one calling me. I ran out. Papa was coming home from the wood, running—then staggering and nearly falling—then running on again blindly. And he rushed up to me, seized me, and dragged me along with him, crying out : 'Singleton—Singleton—I tell you—send for him! Help me to destroy that will, Haidee—it is unjust—unjust —and I never was unjust.' I declare, Singie, it was the most piteous sight and the saddest cry I ever heard. At last he got to his writing-table and began trying to open it. I helped him—but I was slow, because I was frightened. While I was fumbling with the key, he said in a gentle and altered tone, quiet and earnest : 'It is coming, Haidee—and it is death. O God of heaven, give me five minutes, that I may do justice to my son !'"

"O Haidee! thank Heaven for that! my poor, poor father."

"Then I got the table open and he pulled out a drawer, and dragged out a paper. He was going to tear it, when he fell at my feet."

"Not dead though !"

"Not dead, but he never spoke plainly again. He asked for you, but his mind was quite astray, and on the third day he had another stroke and died."

"It was a dreadful time for you, Haidee."

"O Singleton, it was worse at the last than I can tell you. I thought I should have died of the disappointment. He had been getting stronger and his mind evidently clearer. And he tried so hard to say something—something about you. And I never left him, night nor day, lest he might say it and not to me. Phillips was in the room, and Pierce, for I could trust Pierce and kept him for safety—for really I was frightened sometimes. Papa began to speak, and I thought, more coherently; and Pierce told me afterwards that Phillips noticed this and at once left the room. He came back, bringing John, who had never showed himself in the room before. My father saw John, and he suddenly sat up. 'You scoundrel!' he cried, 'you villain! where is Black James?' Singleton, I can swear that those were his words; but the effort was too much for him, and he fell back dying."

"But what had made my father—what had he found out?"

"We have made out—Mr. Seldon and I— that John and Phillips must have been talking in the oak wood. He must have overheard enough to open his eyes. John was on the road to Plymouth with Phillips, on foot, when the groom passed them on his way for a doctor, and told them that Sir Lionel was dying. Then I suppose they ventured back on the chance that he might never speak again."

"Did any one except yourself hear what my father said?"

"John must have heard. Pierce did not, and Phillips says he did not, of course. Singleton, I am afraid we are not a bit the better of it."

"I fear not, except that I'm glad my poor father knew the truth. And the will is to be read to-morrow?"

"Yes. And I am very much afraid that all our mother's money goes to John."

"Let it go. It will not prosper with him. The dear old place must be mine, and that is enough for you and me."

She looked up quickly at him, but he said no more.

"Tell me about yourself, Singleton. Shall you go to sea again?"

"No. The service is no place for me. I was glad to stay with the dear old Captain, and thought myself lucky when he got me appointed; but I have been as lonely among them all as you have been here, Haidee. John had taken care to spread the story; half of them believed me mad, and the other half believed me a murderer; and afterwards, when, perhaps, it might have been forgotten, I could not forget, and kept my distance. But Captain Hamilton's kindness I never can forget."

"And was he the *only* one?"

"No," Singleton answered, his face brightening; "Paddy O'Hara wrote me such a kind letter, saying he did not and would not believe a word against me. Dear old Paddy!"

"I shall love him for ever!" exclaimed Haidee.

"I don't suppose he would have any objection to that, my dear," replied Singleton. "But by the way, where is Phillips?"

"He went with John. Whatever John gets, you may be sure Phillips is to have half of it. Mr. Seldon has tried again and again to bribe him."

"It is of no use, Haidee. I feel quite certain poor old James is dead; and I must make up my mind to be—as I am, all the days of my life."

The reading of Sir Lionel's will took place next day. John did not appear in person, but sent a solicitor from Plymouth to represent him. Mr. Seldon brought with him the will of which he had had the keeping; but the one which the poor deceived man had tried to destroy was of much later date, and perfectly legal and formal. It left nothing whatever to Haidee, and nothing to Singleton that he could be deprived of. All went to "my dear cousin John Trelawney, who has for many years been to me as a son." It left Singleton a tolerably rich man, however; and Haidee was not likely to want while he had plenty. Mr. Seldon was furious at the injustice, and spoke of disputing the will as unnatural; but neither the brother nor the sister would hear of it. So John Trelawney triumphed at last, and Sir Singleton began his reign at the Abbey, a poorer man than he ought to have been, and with the dark shadow of disgrace still hanging over him. He had a long conversation with Mr. Seldon, who was very anxious to prove to him that he had done everything in his power to find Black James.

"You could not have done more, Mr. Seldon. I begin to think the poor old fellow must be dead. Nothing on earth would have kept him from giving himself up if he had an idea that the blame of his act had fallen upon me. Now, my only hope is, that John and his precious accomplice may fall out, and that won't happen until the money is spent."

"I shall try to see Phillips and give him to understand that I shall reward him handsomely when he feels disposed to help us," said Mr. Seldon. "And now, good-bye, Sir Singleton—the only comfort is that you are safe enough now—and even that is something."

CHAPTER X.

AGAIN the brother and sister sat by the fire in the drawing-room, Singleton in the same great chair, Haidee close beside him. It was the same hour too, as when on the evening before they had what Haidee called "their very first comfortable talk together,"—"and I am ready for another now, Singie. I declare I've had no one to talk to for so long that my tongue is out of practice—and you have grown very silent, do you know?"

"I dare say I have, but I feel pretty sure that we shall improve with practice. Haidee, you have had a dreadful time of it these four years."

"Yes—it has been bad enough. But the worst of it was, having nothing to do. When one is miserable, real hard work would be such an unspeakable comfort. I wanted to have schools and classes, and indeed they are sadly wanted here, for I assure you the people are in a bad way; but Dimmock persuaded papa that my interference would do some mysterious mischief—and then papa declared he would have nothing of the kind attempted, and John kept him to it, that more money might be saved for him."

"Well, my dear, you shall have enough to do in that line now! a year hence, you will be crying out for mercy, and a few hours to yourself. I have been studying the subject—Captain Hamilton, dear old boy, always so wise and sensible, advised me to read so as to fit myself for my future work. He saw I was taking to reading, and that the navy was 'too hot to hold me.'"

"And you'll be your own steward, or whatever Dimmock is! O how delightful."

"The very first thing I shall do is to get rid of Dimmock. I do believe that half the evils on the estate are his doing. I have given him warning in fact. And then, Haidee, we'll go in for improvement, hammer and tongs."

He tried to speak with something of his old eagerness, and was under the impression that he was succeeding, when Haidee suddenly burst into tears.

"It won't do, Singie! the old ring is gone

out of your voice, and there is no hope of making me fancy that it is there."

She knelt beside him and laid her soft cheek against his.

"Don't try to take me in, dear. Let us comfort one another—there is nothing gained by pretending. Only—one word, Singie. Is it to be only you and I?"

"Who else could there be? we are alone in the world now; perhaps you'd like John as an assistant, Haidee?"

She looked at him steadily, not noticing his question, and said:

"Singleton, I must speak, once for all. Have you ceased to care for Hester?"

"Have I ceased to live?" he asked, with a calm hopelessness in his face which seemed more at home there than the smile he had tried to summon. "No, I have not; but I hope she has ceased to care for me. My love for her has been a kind of happiness to me, but it cannot hurt her if I never see her, and——"

"Don't be a goose, Singleton! Not hurt her if you never go near her! You don't know what you are saying, I think."

"I mean that the mere fact of my loving her cannot injure her, if I keep it to myself."

"No, but the fact that you keep it to yourself will injure her very much indeed—go very near killing her, I think. Singie, I have not mentioned her in my letters lately."

"And so I concluded that she had left off caring for me."

"And believed all that pretty story of you, I hope? the one is as likely as the other."

"No—she would never believe that. She knew the truth; but I know that her family would do all they could to keep her from thinking of me—and I have not been able to clear myself, you know."

"Well, my dear, her family have done nothing of the kind. They never even tried! and when about a year ago she refused a very good offer, they never interfered."

"What reason did she give?" asked Singleton, shading his face with his hand.

"None, to them. I suppose she gave him a reason which he thought conclusive, for he appeared no more. Well, Singleton?"

"Well, Haidee? She might have had fifty reasons without a thought of me. Suppose she is content and happy and—why, what can I offer her? Disgrace, and to bury her alive here! They would send me about my business, and serve me right."

There was another pause: then Haidee

pulled away his hand and looked at him keenly.

"You *have* ceased to care for her as you did, Singie. After all, you saw very little of her, and there's nothing about her—though she's as good as gold—to make you faithful all this time. She is not beautiful, or striking in any way."

His cheeks crimsoned, and a sudden flash came from his eyes; he sprang up and began pacing the room.

"Not striking!" he said. "O Haidee, if you only knew her! My gentle, trusting, loving Hester! type of true womanhood—born consoler and strength-giver. Haidee, I could be very angry with you."

"Could you really? and why?"

"What does a woman want with being striking?" he went on. "Winning—stealing into your very life and being part of it for ever—that's what Hester is. Ah, if I were only sure that she would be happier as my wife than as she is! I would have her if she had fifty fathers."

"Yes, my dear; and now that you have fussed and fumed about enough, come here and sit down again. You dear stupid old fellow—I thought I should make you speak out. Now, Singleton, listen to me. Hester loves you with all her heart. She'll never leave off, so you need not think it. If you make believe to have forgotten her, according to your self-denying little nonsense, she will not say one word of blame, but I think she might die of it."

"How do you know this?—are you sure, Haidee? She was so young—four years is such a long time."

"Ah, ha! I've roused you at last. How do I know? I know because—she—told me."

"When?" exclaimed Singleton, turning to her, with no want of animation about him now.

"The last time she was here. I was writing to you, and she said, 'Tell him I am with you.' I answered: 'I never name you to him now.' So she asked why. I said because you never mentioned her. 'And you think he has forgotten me,' she said, and laughed. 'Men *do* forget,' I answered. 'But he will not,' she said quietly, 'nor shall I; it may be years and years, but he will find me just the same. I have his letter here,' and she showed me a little case with the letter in it, hung round her neck by a ribbon; 'and I shall keep it until he comes back to me.' So I asked: 'Does mamma know this?' 'They all know it. I have told them that when he asks me I shall marry him, and that I shall never marry any one else.' I said no more, for I did not feel as certain of you as she did—and it seems I did you an injustice."

Again Singleton sprang to his feet.

"Come along and pack up, old woman. We'll be off to London to-morrow—you'll come and help me, Haidee, won't you? no, you don't wish to come—I forgot—forgive me, dear Haidee, I was a brute to say that. But I shall go—and if matters stand as you say—and surely you wouldn't cheat me—we'll have my Hester—my darling—here with us; and who could be unhappy then, I should like to know?"

Haidee said no more that night, but when he was ready to start early next day, she appeared, also ready.

"I thought it better to go, Singleton. I could give you twenty excellent reasons, but one will do. I *can't* lose sight of you again so soon."

"But you know, dear, who—may be there?"

"I do know, I rather wish it. I must see him, and when it is over, this first time, I shall not care. I shall not indeed, Singleton."

"O Haidee! how that grieved me."

"Yes, I know it did. But you know he never cared for me—we will not talk about it now. But you may believe me that I am cured of my folly."

Haidee had been so long without leaving home that the journey tired her out, and she was fit for nothing during the rest of that day. But next morning she begged to be allowed to go alone to Russell Square, meaning Singleton to follow. To this he would by no means consent.

"No, no," he said; "altered as you find me, I have not become such a coward as that! I can bear it whatever happens—and I'm not going to let you bear it for me. We may as well go early, in the hopes of finding them alone."

Haidee, who could not help seeing how sensitively he shrank from meeting any one who knew him, was very much vexed, but he was firm, and they went together at about one o'clock. As they mounted the steps before the door of the Hamiltons' house, that door was opened and two persons came out. Reginald Hamilton and Arthur Vane. They met—the two coming up and the others standing transfixed at the top of the steps. To add to the embarrassment, Arthur Vane, in his surprise, shut the door: and so there was no escape. It was a moment of exquisite awkwardness—of more than awkwardness—of keen suffering to three of them; and Mr. Vane, though of course less affected, felt the pain of such a meeting.

Singleton stood perfectly still, his eyes fixed upon the face of the man who once had seemed to him so perfect, and who since they last met had nearly broken his sister's heart. Reginald looked from one to the other, and seemed scarcely conscious of what he was doing. Haidee, who had come there prepared, recovered herself first. She knew Arthur Vane, having seen photographs of him, and forgetting that she had never met him before, she held out her hand, saying steadily in a low voice: "How do you do, Mr. Vane?" Then passing Reginald with a bow, she knocked somewhat feebly at the door. The commonplace sound of the knock seemed to break the spell that bound them all. Reginald started and turned round.

"I beg your pardon," he said. "I thought the door was open." And seizing the knocker, he made the house re-echo with the summons.

Singleton, drawing a long breath, bowed to Mr. Vane — the door opened, and Haidee went in.

"Tell Mrs. Hamilton that Miss Trelawney is here, and Mr. Trelawney," she said. "This way, Singleton — come up to the drawing-room."

She put her hand upon his arm and almost

guided him—for he seemed passive and stupefied. Neither Reginald nor Mr. Vane followed them.

"Haidee, this is what I feared for you."

"It is nothing—it is over now. Now, Singie, rouse yourself and don't let them see that you mind."

"But I do mind—and I'm a bad actor, I fear."

Reginald Hamilton and his father-in-law stood for a few moments in the hall, not knowing what to say to each other. Then Mr. Vane left the house, saying :

"I suppose you will be home to luncheon, Reginald ?"

And when the door closed upon him, Reginald said to the servant who was now coming downstairs again to find her mistress :

"I will tell my mother, Dawson—I know where she is."

He went to his father's little sitting-room, where he had left both father and mother, and called her into the hall.

"Mother, there are visitors in the drawing-room," he said, trying to speak carelessly.

"There's nothing wrong, is there, Reginald ?"

"No, nothing. Your visitors are—Miss Trelawney—and Singleton."

She looked at him sorrowfully.

"And you met them! my poor boy."

Reginald went on quickly:

"What brings them here?"

"I have no means of being certain," she replied.

"But—I tell you, he is there too."

With all his pride to help him, he could only speak in broken gasps.

"Yes. I must go to them now."

"Not yet, mother; you know as well as I do what he comes for. He has come to see Hester."

"He has not said so yet, Reginald; and I would rather not discuss it until I am certain."

"Good Heavens, mother! surely no discussion can be necessary. He comes here—a man with such a past—and such a future—to ask you for your daughter, and you speak calmly of discussing it."

"Reginald, be quiet—I can make great allowance for your agitation, but you really must let me judge for myself in this matter."

"Judge—why, his impertinence in coming here at all is so extraordinary that you would be justified in declining to see him."

"I do not wish to decline," she said firmly. "I shall certainly see him, and even if I did not wish to see him I could not hurt my dear Haidee. You know how I love and value her. Let me go now, Reginald—there is nothing gained by this delay."

She passed him as she spoke and went quickly upstairs. Haidee sprang to meet her, but neither of them could speak for some time.

"Mamma! *you* won't be cruel to him—you always liked him, and I am quite sure you don't believe a word they say against him. You know why he is here—don't be cruel to him."

"It does not quite rest with me—but you know I cannot refuse you anything, my darling child. Singleton—I have had eyes and thoughts for nothing but my child here until now; but I am truly glad to see you again."

Singleton looked up—and as their eyes met, she felt that hers were filling fast with tears. He had always had a pleading expression in his eyes, but there was a look in them now which would have melted a harder heart than Mrs. Hamilton could boast of.

"May I hope, Mrs. Hamilton?"

"Hope what?" she asked, half smiling.

But he could not smile: it was far too serious a matter for smiling, with him. He hesitated, stammered, and finally looked to Haidee for help; but that wise woman held her tongue. So he recovered himself with a great effort, and said:

"I think you know what I hope—or would hope if I dared. Perhaps I ought to have asked for Mr. Hamilton, but Haidee told me that he is often not strong enough to bear any agitation."

"He is pretty well to-day. Will you see him at once, or will you make me your messenger?"

"But will you be a friendly messenger? You and he sent me away four years ago, saying: 'Clear yourself of these charges, and then perhaps we may listen to you.' I have not cleared myself: indeed, to be quite truthful I do not see much hope that I ever shall; and yet here I am, asking you to hear me plead my cause. Asking to see Hester—asking if she loves me well enough still in spite of absence, time, calumny and doubt, disgrace and loss of position, to be my wife. And I think you must see that after a complete separation of four weary years, not even a message during most of that time, if I still say I want Hester, and she still says that she loves me—I think you must confess that our love is no light surface feeling that will pass away, but true, real love: the kind of love that God meant when He said : 'What God hath joined let not man put asunder.' And it gives me a right to speak, and her a right to hear."

His voice would have given pathos to a weaker plea; but what struck Mrs. Hamilton most was the quiet manliness of his manner, so much less impulsive than of old. She answered gently :

"I acknowledge your right, Singleton, and Hester's too. And I will be a friendly messenger — you may trust me. Hester is out, gone to see Arabel, but she will soon be home. Haidee, come with me, for Henry won't answer any questions till he has seen you. You don't know how often he has longed for a sight of you, my dear."

Mrs. Hamilton, when she made this proposal, believed that her son had left the house when she parted from him; but Reginald, restless and miserable, had gone back into the study, and was there still. He found his father dozing, and sat down to wait and see what would happen next : and the next thing that happened was that Hester came softly in with her hat in her hand, and seeing him, stopped short, and wondered what was the matter with him.

" You here, Regie ! ˙ Is papa asleep ?"

"Yes—he has been talking a good deal. Uncle Arthur was here, and I think he tired my father."

"Well, Regie—let me congratulate you. I have not seen you since your election."

"Don't congratulate me, Hester. I am beset on all sides with congratulations—and really I care very little about it: it will be something to do, that's all."

"Why, I thought to get into Parliament was your ambition even when you were a boy!" Hester answered wonderingly. Ah yes! but he could have told her that sometimes a wish fulfilled is but a care the more. Reginald Hamilton was rich, prosperous, and in a fair way to be a man of mark. And he was moreover an unhappy and a discontented man.

"How are Marian and the children?"

"All well," he answered shortly. "Why don't you come to see my little girls sometimes, Hester? you are always with Arabel's children. Yet mine are as near to you as hers, and want a little love quite as much," he finished hastily.

Hester could not give him her true reason for not cultivating a friendship with his two little girls, peevish, spoiled little creatures, with tempers sorely tried by alternate neglect and indulgence on their mother's part. Marian disliked her and was absolutely rude to her unless Reginald was present, so that visits to his house were far from pleasant. But she only answered:

"Arabel is always glad of a little help, you know. Where is mamma?"

"Upstairs—there are visitors."

Something in his voice made her look quickly at him.

"Who are they, Regie?"

"I have not been upstairs," he replied after a moment's pause.

"I think I shall go to her. Papa will doze now till luncheon-time and will not want me."

"No, no; stay here. My mother will—you don't see me so often, Hester, that you need run away from me. Do not go now."

Hester was looking at him, and he coloured as he met her eyes.

"Reginald, tell me who is upstairs?"

They seemed to have changed characters—her soft, brown eyes were full of a quiet determination; his usually calm, proud face looked strangely embarrassed and undecided.

"You need not answer me," she said after a moment: "it is—Haidee. I have been wondering why she did not write, and——" Her face lost its gentle composure, and brightened as if a sunbeam had suddenly rested upon it. " And, O Regie! is he there too?"

" Hush! don't rouse my father. Yes, Hester, he is there too. I met them at the door, and I ought to have gone away, but I could not—I wanted, if possible, to say one word to you, Hester—I warn you. It is no time for false modesty. We know what brings him here, and I must warn you, even if it angers you; for I fear no one else will. Hester, as surely as you are standing there and I here, Singleton fired that shot at his father. I was there soon afterwards, and spared no pains to sift the story thoroughly. I had no wish to believe it, Heaven knows! it was misery to me to believe it; but I could find no shadow of an excuse for doubt. I don't know what you believe about his sanity—I don't know what to believe myself about it; but sane or insane, the woman who would be rash enough to marry him will wreck her own life, and entail misery and disgrace upon her children. No one will say this to you if I don't—they are all blinded—but it is my duty to warn you, and to tell you plainly that I can never look upon him but as a disgraced man."

She raised her hand, and stopped him there.

" No more, Reginald! you have said enough, and more than enough. Now, listen to me.

Perhaps I ought not to speak as if certain that he comes here for me, but I am certain of it, and I will speak as plainly as you have spoken. I believe him to be perfectly innocent of all that has been laid to his charge. The world, misled by John Trelawney, poor Sir Lionel, and by you, Regie—by *you!* may believe otherwise; but those who know him — those who have hearts to understand him, will believe as I do. I shall be proud to share his sorrow now, and his triumph when it comes; but not more proud of my share of the triumph than that I helped to bear the sorrow. And this because I love him, Reginald! This is love—a feeling which I fear you know little of. Oh, I could forgive all the rest, but how can I forgive—how can I forget, that among the first to fall away from him—to believe any one rather than himself— was the man he had loved so unselfishly, and for whose happiness he sacrificed himself!"

In her agitation, Hester never perceived that she had awakened her father, who was listening to her in much amazement; nor were any of them aware that Haidee and Mrs. Hamilton had come into the room. There was a screen before the door, and hearing Hester's quiet voice a little raised, they had paused to listen. Haidee whispered:

"He is there—we must meet, mamma, and I am glad to meet him thus." And she passed on into the room just as Hester ceased to speak. Mr. Hamilton rose with unwonted haste to meet her.

"My dear, dear child! my dear Haidee!" And he held her fondly in his arms and kissed her. "You don't know how glad I am to see you, little girl. I was only half awake and could not understand what they were saying. I had no idea you were here."

Haidee turned to speak to Hester, but the place where that young lady had lately stood was vacant, save that her hat lay upon the floor. In the pause which ensued, the drawing-room door was distinctly heard to open and shut. Haidee looked from one to the other, and in spite of her agitation and embarrassment, she could hardly help laughing. Mrs. Hamilton was trying to look as if she did not know what that closing door meant. Mr. Hamilton was unfeignedly puzzled by his daughter's rapid flight, and Reginald stood with downcast eyes and set lips, his sister's words ringing in his ears, and the woman he had loved—alas! he knew now, if till now he had not known, that he loved her still—close to him, yet so far from him; welcomed by his father as his wife never had been welcomed and never would be ; lovely and loving as ever—but not for him.

And Singleton, too, his old friend—Singleton, who had been as a brother to him, and was soon to be his brother, though not as he once hoped ; hard as he had striven to steel his heart against this friend of old times, he could not be under the same roof with him without a keen pang of pain. And he had seen him—did he look like a cowardly assassin ? or like a madman ? And if his father and mother were really convinced of his innocence ? But Reginald Hamilton was, as we have seen before, a slave to his own expressed opinion. Even as he stood there, and these thoughts swept over his mind like a storm, yet with a marvellous strength his will clung to the old belief. *He* had inquired carefully, and had been convinced, unwillingly convinced, that Singleton was guilty. Who had such reason as he for wishing to believe otherwise ? Had he not sacrificed his happiness because he could not disguise his conviction ? Nothing had changed since then—four years had passed without any further light being thrown upon the affair. His father and mother, loving Haidee and Hester dearly, were like other people, willing to be blind, ready to be deceived ; but it was not so with him. He could no more help seeing the truth than he could consent to disguise it — the man was guilty and disgraced, and he would give no countenance to Hester's folly. All this flashed through his mind like lightning, and if he had wavered for a second, no one knew it—not even himself. He came forward after that moment's pause, placed a chair for Haidee, and said to his father:

"I was waiting until you awoke, sir, to say good-bye. Mother, let me speak to you in the hall for a moment." Then there was a momentary quiver of the proud lip as he added: "Good-bye, Miss Trelawney."

She held out her hand, and even smiled—a bright, cold smile that meant nothing. And he knew how she *could* smile. So they met: and so they parted.

"Mother," he said, when the door was shut between him and Haidee, "do you mean to let this go on?"

"I do, Reginald. As far as my good word will help him, he shall have it. Hester is neither a baby nor a fool—she has a perfect right to decide for herself, and as you are aware she has decided."

"It seems then that there is no use in my speaking: and yet, remember, I made every effort to discover the truth, and could not find the least reason for doubt. I know you think that I—that I have no right to speak; but whether you approve of my conduct or not, in common honesty I must say this much."

"Let us talk no more about it, Reginald."

"As you will, mother; but I want to make you quite understand that thinking as I do, I will not meet him; nor notice him in any way."

"I think you don't know how much pain you will give Hester—but I will not discuss it—do as you choose. I can only hope that the day will come that even you must be convinced of his innocence."

He looked round suddenly—he had reached the door, and paused with his hand upon the lock.

"If that day were to come, I should go mad. Mother! have you no idea of what it would mean to me? But it is childish folly to talk of it—Good-bye, mother! I shall trouble you with no further interference."

"My poor Regie," murmured Mrs. Hamilton. "People call Singleton's a wrecked life, and yours a prosperous one! but your wreck is far more complete than his."

She went back into the study, and found that Haidee had made good use of her time.

" Hester, I suppose you know what this little girl has been saying to me ?"

" I suppose I do. And as I know you have not the heart to vex her—why, I may hold my tongue."

" Do you hear that, Madam Haidee ? But, however, even for you, my dear girl, I could not let my daughter marry your brother, if I believed all these stories of him. But the plain fact is, that I don't ! The last time I spoke about it was to Arthur Vane ; and he told me candidly that any one but a fool must see that he was guilty, but I never set up for a Solon. I was startled at first and doubtful—his explanation about the debts was wild ; but when I had time to think, I knew I should have done it myself, at his age."

" I am sure you would !"

" I'm not certain that that's a compliment, Haidee, but it was meant to be, no doubt."

" It is a compliment ! You can understand him, because you too would have been capable of a headlong, uncalculating generosity, which some people don't believe in because they never felt it."

" Just so ! very nicely explained. And I have another reason for giving my consent, Haidee."

"And what is that, Mr. Hamilton?"

"Well you see, that young Hester of ours looks as gentle and meek as a girl can look—but she is of a very obstinate disposition, and if I enacted the cruel parent, it would be a case of 'She's o'er the border and awa'' some fine morning. And so, Haidee!——"

"And so you mean to be the dear, kind father you always are! But you used to like Singleton, Mr. Hamilton—you will be kind to him, won't you? You don't know how he needs it. He is so changed—for the better in many ways; but indeed he wants all the love and kindness his few *real* friends can show him, to make him believe that he has any friends left."

"Like him—of course I liked him. As my sister Jane Seymour says, he is simply the most fascinating person I ever met. But as to friends —Frank stood by him, didn't he?"

"Frank—oh! Captain Hamilton, you mean? Indeed he did. He has always treated Singie as if he were his son."

"His son! Yes—no doubt," answered Mr. Hamilton with a smile, and also with a sigh. "Ah, little Haidee. Time brings strange changes, my dear. I shall never be surprised to hear that Frank leaves off treating him as a son, and promotes him—tries to promote him I should say—to the rank of brother."

"What do you mean? What *does* he mean, mamma?"

"He is talking nonsense, my dear. Henry, you ought to be ashamed of yourself."

"My dear, I *cannot* be blind."

"No, but you *can* be silent—you may do harm, and besides—Henry, I can't bear it."

Her voice failed, and she turned away to hide her face; poor Reginald's face of defiant misery was before her, and her heart was full of him. Haidee looked from one to the other, and wondered what on earth they meant. She told herself that she had no idea what it could be, and so I suppose she had not; but there was a very brilliant colour in her cheeks, which was not always there now.

"All this time, where is Hester?" inquired Mr. Hamilton.

Haidee laughed mischievously.

"Ah, yes—where can she be? There's her hat—and she was here herself a little while ago."

"My dear Henry—to tell you the truth, I think she is in the drawing-room."

"Well, why does she not come here? What took her to the drawing-room when Haidee is here?"

"Because—you see, Singleton is there!"

"Oh the audacious little sinner! So while I was debating the question here, Miss Hester has been settling it for herself upstairs. I've a good mind to give her a fright."

"No, no, don't be spiteful, Mr. Hamilton. You can't frighten Hester without frightening Singleton too, and I shall not allow that."

"Then run upstairs, like a good girl, and bring the culprits before me. Tell your brother I would gladly go to him, but I cannot manage those stairs now at all."

"Now you are to be *very* kind to him. Oh, dear Mr. Hamilton! for my sake, pretend you are very glad. Surely he has suffered enough."

CHAPTER XI.

To return to Singleton. When he was left alone in the great, comfortable drawing-room, he looked round, naturally enough, for some signs of Hester's frequent presence; and in a moment his quick eyes found out a little work-basket lined with blue silk, which he well remembered. In fact, he had often been told that he was very troublesome for pulling the contents about while he talked to its owner. He was still looking lovingly at the insensible basket, which remained quite calm and unmoved, when he heard quick, light steps upon the stairs. In another moment Hester came in. He never asked a question, or said a word, but met her as she came toward him; took her hand, looked into her clear eyes, heaved a great sigh of perfect satisfaction, and took her to his heart—for ever. There was no need for words. They were together: they would part no more till parted by the will of Heaven.

And in half a minute—so it seemed to them—Haidee came in.

" Haidee, you were right."

" I always am, dear."

" O Haidee, how good you were to bring him so soon," whispered Hester, clinging to her.

" I was — very good," Haidee answered, laughing, but with a sob in the midst of the laugh; " for I was sorely tempted to keep him to myself for just a little while."

" But he will be none the less yours because I am there too, Haidee."

" I know that—I want you, Hester; but sorrow and disappointment make one sadly selfish."

" They have not made you selfish," Singleton said, kissing her. " I think, now, I am possessed of the two very best women in the world. But what do they say--what does Mr. Hamilton say, Haidee ?"

" He says he wants to see you, but cannot come upstairs, so you are to come to him. I will show you the way, for I don't think Hester knows what she is doing."

They went down to the study.

" Here they are, Mr. Hamilton, and I am

afraid they are by no means in a penitent frame of mind."

"I should be penitent, sir," said Singleton, "only I am too happy. I had hardly dared to hope. You know you sent me away until I could prove that I was speaking the truth, and I have come back just as I went—and yet——"

"Well, Singleton, let us talk it over now, and be done with it. I confess I was doubtful of you then. I never actually believed it all; but I doubted, and above all, I feared that there might be some truth in the assertion that you were mad. Your poor father had once told me that he suspected it, and I wavered in my first conviction, which was that he did not understand you. But I have long felt certain that your version of the story was true."

"Oh, papa! why did you not tell me so? It would have made me so happy."

"But, my child, he might have forgotten you; four years is a long time. But as you are both of the same mind, I have no right, and believe me, Singleton, I have no wish, to stand in the way. Only, don't quite rob us of her—we cannot afford to lose another altogether."

"Indeed I will not, sir. I should be the most ungrateful hound on earth if I forgot your kindness," Singleton exclaimed, with something of his old animation.

There was no reason for delay, and there were reasons against it. Under the circumstances it was better to give but little time for gossip. So Singleton and Hester were quietly married, and went down to the Abbey, where they were joined in a week by Haidee.

It had been a very quiet wedding. Except Mrs. Seymour, not one of the Hamiltons' friends and relations either congratulated the bride, or was present at the marriage. This was principally owing to Reginald's conduct; for, true to his declaration that he would have nothing to say to the affair, he took his family back to Heronhurst, and remained there until the wedding was over. This naturally set everybody talking, and but for this the scandal about Singleton would probably have been utterly forgotten, in London at least; though not, of course, in his own neighbourhood. Mrs. Seymour was as kind as she could be, and assured her brother that if he had refused his consent, she would have assisted Hester to elope with her lover. "A little real true love, my dear, is so refreshing in these prosaic days; and you'll find that Hester will be the happiest woman in the world. I mean to visit the Abbey every summer."

So London ignored Sir Singleton Trelawney,

and Devonshire sent him to Coventry. His wife and sister, however, seemed very happy, and Haidee began to look like her bright self once more.

After a while Mr. and Mrs. Hamilton came to the Abbey, for a month, Mr. Hamilton said: and he was always talking of going home, but somehow, time slipped away and found him still at the Abbey. Sir Lionel's rooms had been refurnished for him, and all his likings and dislikings so carefully attended to, that he felt at home at once. Mrs. Hamilton had no wish to move. Arabel's husband had accepted a living at a great distance from London, so that city held no attraction now for her. Besides, she had been seriously hurt by William Hastings' refusal to perform the ceremony, or to allow Arabel to be present at the wedding. Nevertheless, thinking as he did, I do not know that the young clergyman could have acted otherwise.

One source of Haidee's happiness (and that she was happy none could doubt who saw her youth and beauty reviving like flowers after rain) was that she was now provided with plenty of very congenial employment. She was a young woman of a very practical turn of mind, and what are called "lady-like accomplishments," when considered as the serious business of life, appeared to her a mere waste of time. But when her music helped her to train the choir for Singleton's pretty Church, built on the site of the Lady Chapel, in fulfilment of his ancient vow; and when her knowledge of drawing enabled her to detect and assist a rustic genius whom she discovered in the new day-school—then indeed she regarded these arts with much more respect than when they were her only helps to kill time, under her father's iron sway.

Singleton's rule was certainly very different from that which prevailed under Sir Lionel, and the estate gradually changed—from a nest of vice, ignorance and poverty, such as it would surprise any one to find in England in these days of enlightenment and improvement; a place where ignorant farmers rode rough-shod over more ignorant and utterly helpless labourers; where children grew up untaught, and Sunday was a day for idle mirth, hard drinking, and occasionally for hard fighting as well; where morality was at the lowest ebb, and religion went no further than occasionally moving parents to get a child baptised; where, in the village at least, the dirt fairly rivalled even the dirt of old Ireland—to a tolerably happy, decently ordered and perfectly peaceful community. But it was a change not wrought in a day, nor without much hard work and a good deal of self-denial; for Singleton had no ready money to dispose of, and was too wise to borrow. So he worked slowly, but surely, and did as much by example as by any other means.

And he had many trials in the course of his work; trials arising from his peculiar circumstances, of which one instance will give an idea.

Of course there were many, in the little village particularly, who resented all the new ideas and resisted every change that was proposed, as far as they could. Old Dimmock, Sir Lionel's very dishonest steward, naturally headed the malcontents. He had been pensioned off, although Singleton would have been justified in dismissing him ignominiously; but he would not do it, lest he might seem to throw blame upon his father, who had always upheld the excellent Dimmock. But if he had met with his deserts, instead of getting a good pension, Dimmock could not have been more disgusted; and instead of going away as every one hoped he would, he took a small house in the village and remained there doing all the mischief he could, and being very insolent to Singleton whenever they met.

Until the church was finished, Divine Service was held in the large new schoolroom in the village ; and " the family " made every effort to get the people to attend. (Until now the nearest church had been four miles off.) The farmers, among whom not even Singleton's " new-fangled notions" could make him unpopular, attended to please him, but the men of the village seemed generally to prefer the public-house. However, after a time the landlord of the public house was prevailed upon by Singleton, who threatened to turn him out if milder measures failed, to close his house on Sundays —to close it in good earnest, I mean ; for nominally it had always been closed, at least during part of the day. Still the greater part of the men did not come to church, and old Dimmock, simply to annoy Singleton, invited them to spend the time of service in his parlour, where much drinking went on. At last, one Sunday evening there was a terrible row, which began in Dimmock's house, but soon overflowed into the street : so that when the church-goers were leaving the school-house, they found themselves in the midst of a free fight. While Singleton was piloting Hester and Haidee through the crowd a voice called out :

" There'll be murder here in another minute."

Singleton turned to see what was going on. The one policeman who represented the majesty of the law was trying hard to rescue a feeble-looking old man from the clutches of a strong young ruffian, who was evidently too drunk to know what he was doing. Singleton sent his ladies home, called up Pierce and the other servants, who with the two or three gardeners made quite a formidable force, and having rescued the poor old man, quickly put an end to the fighting. But the old man was badly injured, and the solitary policeman had been hustled and insulted, and so the matter came before the magistrates. With all his shrinking from public places, Singleton could not avoid going to give his evidence: and as people were naturally curious to see him and had but few opportunities of doing so, the magistrates' room was crowded. The man was convicted on Singleton's testimony, and when during the examination, he saw that his conviction was certain, he remarked aloud in an insolent voice:

"Sir Singleton wasn't allays so pertickler, for sure! and if so be as I did hit old Matt Ellery, I didn't shoot he from behind a holly bush—and he bein't my *father* neither."

There was a dead silence. Then one of the magistrates said :

"Prisoner, if you interrupt the proceedings again, you won't make your sentence any lighter."

Singleton finished his evidence calmly and went home. He said nothing about it, even to Hester: but she knew well enough that something had occurred to distress him: and it was not wonderful that he seldom left his own domains.

One good result of this affair was, that it rid the village of the three worst characters in it, for Dimmock was obliged to depart, Singleton's patience being exhausted, Bill Jenkins never returned after his term of imprisonment was over, and old Ellery never quite recovered his strength, and moreover became a zealous supporter of "Sir Singleton—who carried me as if I'd been his best friend, and spoke so gentle and kind-like."

But the Abbey was not wholly without visitors. Mrs. Seymour kept her promise, and spent a month there pretty often; and Paddy O'Hara was a constant visitor, until one unlucky day he confessed to Haidee that he loved her and had loved her ever since his first pleasant visit long ago. Haidee was very much grieved, but refused him decidedly. Singleton pled his friend's cause with much eloquence, but she would not hear.

"I *cannot*, Singleton. I have been so miserable—I am happy now. Let me alone, if you love me."

"Don't bother her," said the generous Irishman. "I'll get over it, Singleton. But I do sometimes wish I had poor Hamilton in the middle of the big bog on my father's place—and no one by! If she had married him and been happy, I'd never have complained; but to see a woman like her, with her life spoiled for his diversion—that does provoke me. But I won't bother her, nor let you bother her about me. She says no, and she means it; and I'll take my answer and be off, as a gentleman ought."

And Francis Hamilton came and went, making the Abbey his home for the greater part of the year, and devoting himself to Haidee's service in a manner which certainly contributed very much to her recovery—as it may truly be called, though she had not been actually ill. Whether she saw what his feelings were, no one could tell. He thought that she did, and meant by her gentle friendly manner to show that she did not wish to hear more of them, so he said nothing. Occasionally he spoke of going to sea again, but nothing came of it, except perhaps a visit to Mrs. Seymour. Then

Haidee would write, telling him of some approaching school feast, or something of that kind, the preparations for which imperatively required his presence : and he would return, nothing loath. So the years went on—and Hester had first a little girl and then a boy; and after the birth of the boy, Singleton seemed to feel his disgrace with tenfold bitterness. He grew thin and pale ; and his strength failed so much that his many employments became very arduous to him. But he never complained, nor spoke about it except once to Hester ; and then only because she found him gazing at the boy with such a sad look that she could not refrain from saying :

"Singleton ! you must not think that !"

"Think what, my wise woman," he said, trying to smile.

"You are thinking it always—' Will this child grow up to believe all the stories against me ?' And how *could* he believe them ? He will grow up seeing your useful, loving life, and taught by all around him to love and value you, And mind, he is *my* son. How could *my* son fail to love and understand you ?"

"Hester—I did not mean you to know : but oh, I feel now that I did wrong in marrying you."

"How can you say that to me? I should have broken my heart if you had not come back to me. Ah, Singie, have a little faith. The truth will come out yet."

"Seven years and six months now. No, Hester, I have given up hope of that. My faith must be, not that I shall be cleared of this—but that it is good for us all, though I cannot see it."

"Singie, it has been good for you. And what is good for you must be good for us, who are yours. Only don't think evil of my boy—I know he will think there is no one in the world half so good as my good husband—and he will be quite right."

Singleton stooped and kissed the fair blue-eyed baby and said:

"God bless him—and you, my comforter. I believe I cannot repent of having married you, Hester."

All this time the only news they had of Reginald was from his own letters to his mother, and Mrs. Seymour's reports of Marian's sayings and doings in town. He had lately accepted a post under Government, the offer of which proved that he was already a man of some mark; and his ambition seemed likely to be gratified by a very successful career. But Mrs.

Seymour said that he looked stern and anxious, and that Marian was simply the greatest flirt she had ever met with, and the most extravagant woman in London. Mr. Vane had died during the year after Singleton's return, and from something said by Marian, Mrs. Seymour had come to the conclusion that Reginald had been very much disgusted to find that two months spent at Heronhurst, with a few chosen friends to keep her company, and the most ornamental mourning worn for a year, was all the tribute his wife saw fit to pay to the memory of her most kind and loving father.

"They are a very fashionable couple, my dear; seldom seen together! But no doubt Reginald will be a great man one of these days, and as he seems devoted to his work, I suppose we may hope that he is not unhappy."

No one answered Mrs. Seymour's remark, or echoed her hope. They knew him too well to hope that he was happy.

When four years had come and gone, Francis Hamilton "tried his luck," as he called it, with Haidee, who wept abundantly, and asked him pathetically "how he *could* say such things to her?" She refused him, but begged him to forget that he had spoken, and to remain at the Abbey. To which he replied:

"No, Haidee. I've tried my best to win you, and you are not to be won by me, at all events. What made me speak was, that I have been offered a ship, and I shall accept it. I cannot stand this life any more; I am no boy, to live on hopes and fears, and kind words that mean nothing."

"That mean nothing!" she echoed reproachfully.

"Nothing *but* kindness; nothing that I want them to mean. I have loved you all your life, Haidee. I loved you, I think, before he did, and I can't leave off now, I am sorry to say. But I can go away; and I will."

And he did, meaning in his heart to see the Abbey no more. But not long afterwards, while fitting out his ship at Devonport, he met with a severe accident. A rope broke, and the flying end scattered men and officers like ninepins; one or two were killed, and Captain Hamilton was severely injured. Singleton went to the Naval Hospital as soon as he heard of this accident, and never left his captain night or day until he was out of danger, and could be removed to the Abbey, the doctors said, with great care.

"No, no, Singleton! the Abbey is no place for me. I am an old fool, and—I have no hope now."

"You just let me be Captain this once, Captain Hamilton. Haidee did little but cry for a fortnight after you left us, and I thought she was going to faint when we heard of your mishap. You come home with me and let us nurse you, and just see what will come of it. Poor old Haidee! she's afraid of the very idea of being married, I believe. This is Hester's advice, you must know."

"Hester must be obeyed, I suppose," replied the Captain, and offered no further resistance to his fate.

So he was brought back to the Abbey, and was received with tears of sympathy and many blushes. But for some time he was too ill to think of anything but his pains and aches.

CHAPTER XII.

ONE sultry evening in July Reginald Hamilton left the House of Commons alone. Weary with the heat and noise, and finding that the air refreshed him, he determined to walk part of the way home. He was in no haste; his dinner hour was half-past eight, and it was now only seven: the Abbey bells were ringing for Evensong, and people were going in. The thought of the cool space and lofty pillars was pleasant, and half absently he crossed the space between, and joined the throng who were entering. But he did not enter the Abbey that evening.

Just outside the gate, a man touched him on the shoulder, causing him to look round. This man had been watching him ever since he began to walk towards the Abbey, with somewhat doubtful eyes. A tall old negro, whose woolly hair was almost white, his form bent and infirm, his step tottering and uncertain, his eyes bloodshot and wild. But in spite of the change from the well-dressed, respectable looking servant, to this drunken, shabby creature, Reginald knew him at a glance. It was the long-sought Black James.

Hamilton stood like a statue: something which was neither hope nor fear, but made up of both, or which was perhaps excitement merely, and a kind of horror, seemed to paralyze him. The negro stood crouchingly before him; the crowd had passed on. Reginald glanced round, mechanically looking to see if any one had noticed him, but James misunderstood the action, and began in hurried, broken tones:

"Don't do it, Mr. Regie. It is not needed. Don't ye do it, sir."

At the sound of the man's voice Reginald staggered back as if he had been struck.

"Don't call a policeman," persisted James. "For the love of Heaven, help a poor mis-able black fellow; poor ignorant nigger. They have kept me shut up and told me lies for years, Mr. Regie. And when I came to think that, I couldn't live until I knew if I had harmed *him!* But he would spare me if he could—what's the use of punishing poor old Black James? I was mad, Mr. Regie, and the devil whispered to me to do it."

"To do it! to do what?" said Hamilton slowly; then rapidly, "Stop! not a word, don't answer me here. Not here. Is that a cab— Here! get in James."

In a minute more they were rattling over the streets towards Reginald's home. Not a word did either of them speak on the way. The negro seemed partly to forget what was passing, he sat staring out of the window and rolling his eyes vacantly, after the fashion of his race.

As to Reginald, he covered his face with his hands and tried to think. Just Heaven! what was he about to hear. Why, of all men, was he to hear it? What if it should be true, after all, that not Singleton, but this wretched creature, had fired that shot? The very thought made him feel sick and faint. To find that he had wrecked his life—not because he was keen to see the truth and honest in avowing it, but because, as both Haidee and Hester had told him, he did not understand the man he had called his friend; because he had deliberately taken the worst view of all his conduct, refusing to believe his explanations, and accepting any evidence rather than his own.

But this brought back some of the old arguments. After all, a man's own evidence in his own favour ought not to weigh against proved facts, against the evidence of many others, all agreeing with those facts. No—the negro had stolen that sum of money from Sir Lionel's table. John Trelawney had always inclined to think that he had, and he was about to confess to the theft. So Reginald told himself; but he did not believe it in the least.

The cab stopped at his own door. He admitted himself by means of a latch key, and led the negro to his own study. There he sat down and faced his visitor.

"Sit down, James. You look tired; are you ill?"

But the negro preferred to stand, glancing furtively round, and looking more like a stray dog than a human being. Hamilton was quite calm again now: he examined the negro more attentively than at first. The man's clothes, though soiled and dusty, were good : and except that he had no hat, there was no appearance of poverty about him. But he had all the look of an habitual drinker, though sober at that moment.

"James, I suppose you know that you have been searched for everywhere, and a large reward offered for any intelligence of you, ever since you—left the Abbey."

"Yes, Mr. Regie. It doesn't matter much

now. I haven't long to live. Is Miss Haidee here, sir?"

"Here! no. Miss Trelawney is at home—at the Abbey."

James looked puzzled.

"You're married, sir—ain't you?"

"Yes—but not to Miss Trelawney," Reginald answered quickly.

"Not to Miss Haidee! They told me you were: but it was a lie. Then they *have*. been lying to me. Look here, Mr. Regie, I want to know the truth, and I came with you gladly because I thought Miss Haidee was here and would tell me all. Sir, my heart is heavy like lead. Oh, tell me quick for the love of Heaven —did any harm come to Mr. Singleton through what I did?"

"You must first tell me what you did?"

"Don't you know, sir? I thought you knew. I shot Sir Lionel."

Of course. Hamilton had known what was coming. He had lost all that made life dear to him because he would not, or could not, believe this: but from the moment when he recognised Black James, he had known that so it was. He sat quite still. Not the quivering of an eyelash betrayed the agony that filled his heart: but he could not speak again for some time.

Then he said:

"James, sit down. This must be thoroughly sifted. You asked me if any harm came to Mr. Singleton through your act. I tell you yes. He was suspected of it himself, and has never been able to prove that he did not do it."

"What did they do to him?" exclaimed James wildly. "O Mr. Singie! my dear young master that never raised voice or hand to me! what have I done?"

"Nothing was done to him. He was never publicly accused. But his father—and others—always believed it of him. And he is under the suspicion to this day. You must speak out, James; I am sure nothing serious will be done to you after so long a time."

"But I hope they'll hang me, Mr. Regie. They ought! a brute like me, killing myself with drink and letting them fill me with lies. I deserve to be hanged: or worse. Get paper and a pen, sir, and write all down while I say it; for I'm a dying man and may never be able to say it again."

Writing materials lay on the table; and Hamilton wrote word for word what the negro told him. But I need not give the story as it was told then, for it was very tedious and rambling: and besides, it cannot contain much that will be new to any one who has read this book. So I shall tell it in my own way.

When Pierce put the discarded negro on board the *Stars and Stripes* he meant, as he said, to sail in her. But brooding over his wrongs, and drinking freely, he soon changed his mind. He determined to return to the Abbey, see Singleton, and perhaps persuade him to take him as his own servant. With this idea, he went on shore again, just in the hurry and confusion of sailing: walked back to Trelawney Abbey during the night, and concealed himself about the place during the early part of the next day, in the hope of meeting Singleton. While thus prowling about, he came suddenly upon the rifle, leaning against a holly tree. Knowing that it was Singleton's, and that the owner would surely come back for it, he waited among the evergreens, until Sir Lionel came out upon the terrace. Then the remembrance of all that he had patiently borne from his hard and insolent master, and the heartless style of his dismissal, came with new force upon his mind: and the devil (so James declared) whispered to him to shoot him.

Twice he took up the rifle, and laid it down again: but the third time he levelled it and fired. He saw his master stagger, and knew that he was hit : flinging the rifle on the ground he turned and fled, never even perceiving Pierce in pursuit. He went back to Plymouth, through the fields, not daring to walk on the road. Next day Phillips found him out in a small public house in Devonport, and informed him that Singleton had commissioned him to warn him : that Pierce had recognised him, that Sir Lionel was dying, and that if he valued his life he must escape to London, and hide himself in a place of which Jaspar gave him the address, and a note to the proprietor of the house. The terrified negro was a mere tool in Phillips' practised hands, believing him implicitly and obeying him exactly. Phillips procured him a suit of sailor's clothes, and disguised him so skilfully that it was no wonder he was not recognized during the journey. To London he went, and was received into some den of infamy well known to the excellent Jaspar, who visited him from time to time, and paid him a small allowance, which he stated was sent by Singleton: the poor black never doubted the assertion. He was kindly treated, and had every comfort—which meant plenty of gin, which was all he cared for now. This state of things lasted until Sir Lionel's death : but long before that time James had discovered that he was not free to leave the premises; that he was, in fact, a prisoner, though he was assured it was only on his own account that he was thus restrained, as the police were still looking out for him.

At last Phillips came and took him away in a cab. He brought him to a house where they found John Trelawney. Here the negro had lived ever since, but he had no idea in what part of London it was, as he had never been outside the door until the night before he told his story to Reginald Hamilton.

John Trelawney told him that Sir Lionel was dead, having died of the effect of the wound received four years before: that Singleton still wished to protect the old servant, but that as Jaspar Phillips was going to emigrate, it was no longer possible to keep him where he had hitherto lived, and that therefore John had consented to give him an asylum. He was installed in a comfortable room, and was at first kept a close prisoner: but gradually, as John saw how little desire he had to get about, he became free of the house, and when "the Captain" as he still called him, was at home, James acted as his servant. "The Captain" was often away for weeks, but when he was at home the house was full of men and women, who drank and feasted and made merry after a fashion which rather scandalized the negro. However, he had plenty of drink, and was seldom sober, by his own account: and was quite contented.

But at last came a change. Phillips re-appeared upon the scene, very shabby and "down upon his luck," as he said himself. He was coldly received by John, and there was a great quarrel, in the midst of which James walked into the room. Phillips exclaimed:

"Do you mean to say that this old sponge hasn't drunk himself to death yet? and that you let him go about like a tame cat? He'll do you a mischief yet."

John hushed him hurriedly, but the negro had heard enough to make him suspicious. Phillips remained in the house: and quarrels were loud and frequent. He wanted money, and John refused it, saying more than once that he had had more than his share. And once James heard the reply, "If you don't come down with a handsome sum, I'm off to that starched old Seldon to see what that side will bid for me. That young idiot wouldn't be sorry to know the truth, even now, and there is old Woolly-pate ready to confess, if he once got it into his head that the blame had fallen where it did." James, already suspicious, here unfortunately let the speaker see that he was not too drunk to understand what was said, and the worthy pair were in a terrible fright. They locked him up in his room, and John fully intended to keep him there. But in that disorderly household it was not very difficult for the black, who kept himself sober and watched for an opportunity, to escape: which he did, but unfortunately, in getting over the garden wall he fell, and hurt himself a good deal. Between fright, the want of his accustomed stimulants, and his natural dulness, he wandered aimlessly about, hardly knowing where he was: until he saw Reginald Hamilton, and the sight of a face connected with the past brought him to his senses.

Twice during the telling of this story a servant had appeared to say that dinner was ready, and Mrs. Hamilton waiting. The second time this occurred Reginald said:

"Tell your mistress not to wait for me; I am very much occupied and shall not come to dinner."

Now that all was told, he rang the bell.

"Send Jones here. Jones, I leave this person, who was a servant in a house at which I used to visit, in your care. Make him comfortable, and treat him kindly; I don't think he is well, and he ought to have something to eat, and go to bed." Then he whispered: "Don't lose sight of him. It is of consequence that he should be forthcoming."

Jones looked at the negro, who was half asleep, and promised obedience, but seemed unfavourably impressed by his master's acquaintance.

"James, go with my servant. He will see that you are comfortable."

"And you, Mr. Regie—you'll see that my young master is made clear? And will you ask him to come and see me, sir, and forgive me? I never meant *him* any harm, anyhow."

"No, you meant no harm — but Heaven knows you have done harm enough. I will see to it, James, and I think I can promise you your master's forgiveness. It is not you whom he will find it hard to forgive."

The negro roused himself suddenly, and looked keenly at him.

"*You* never believed it, Mr. Regie? You were his friend."

Hamilton turned quickly away.

"Jones, tell your mistress that I am obliged to go out again on business, and cannot be home until rather late."

He was going to Mr. Seldon's office, though with but little hope of finding him there so late; but he felt that he must do something, and this was the first idea that came into his head. He gave himself no time to think, but hurried along as if his life depended on his speed; walking fast appeared in some measure to allay the fever of his mind.

Mr. Seldon was just leaving his office, the clerk said, but would, no doubt, see Mr. Hamilton, as his business was so pressing. So he took him up to the private office at once. Mr. Seldon was in the act of pulling on his boots; a great pile of letters lay on the table, and when he heard the sound of the opening door, he began without looking up:

"Martin, I shall be here very early to-morrow, and if that rascal comes before—Mr. Hamilton! How very extraordinary."

"What is extraordinary? I have that to tell you which will—not surprise you, I believe, but which you will be glad to hear."

"You may go, Martin. Sit down, Mr. Hamilton. What is it?"

"I have found Black James."

"Black James! Then that explains it. The poor old wretch—I wonder where they have kept him. And has he told you all about it?"

"He has; but had he been with you?—you don't seem surprised."

"No, I am not surprised. I always thought he would turn up, though Sir Singleton would have it that he was dead. But the truth is, that audacious scoundrel, calling himself Jaspar Phillips was with me to-day—he has not been long gone—and made a full confession of all that he and Mr. John Trelawney plotted and did. I saw that for some reason or other, he was in a hurry; he so often hinted that a small sum at once would be acceptable, and yet he told me all without getting it. I therefore felt sure that the secret was on the point of coming out. I hope you have the negro safe."

Reginald had sunk into a chair. It was childish and unreasonable, he felt; but his nerves were quite unstrung for the time, and he was bitterly mortified that another witness had appeared, making his discovery of less importance.

"He is safe. He is in my house now. There is his story, or confession, whichever you would call it. I wrote it down exactly as he spoke it, for the old man looks ill, and says himself that he is dying."

"Ah, then we must get a regular witnessed and sworn confession at once. This, you know though very interesting to me, would not do for the public—coming from Sir Singleton's brother-in-law and old friend. Will you let me read it?"

He read it through, smiling pleasantly as he saw how his words had made his visitor redden.

"Yes, so far well. As to the firing at Sir Lionel, we now can dispense with Mr. Phillips, but he only can prove the sending Sir Singleton to that asylum, when he was as sane as I am. John Trelawney ought to be punished; and shall be, if I can manage it."

"Can you touch him?"

"I don't quite know. He managed to keep poor Sir Lionel in the front of the battle so cleverly. Phillips is to be here to-morrow early, and when I have seen him I shall go to the Abbey."

"You will go to-morrow?"

"Yes. I can write if I am delayed, but I shall go if I possibly can. I should like to take Sir Singleton's hand, and tell him that it is all right; that his worst enemy now will have no shadow of excuse for doubting him; that all, however incredulous, must believe him to be what I know him to be—the best, gentlest, most chivalrous gentleman I ever met with."

"Ay, you may wince," was his secret thought. "You may wince, you cold, hard, handsome brute. I'm glad you *can;* and I shan't spare you a pang."

Reginald looked up and met a glance which roused his fiery pride once more to his aid. He rose.

"Well—will you kindly give me back that paper?—thank you. And I am sure you will be very welcome at the Abbey, but I shall be there before you. I shall go by the night train. Good evening, Mr. Seldon."

"Good evening, Mr. Hamilton. I may conclude then, that you acknowledge—that you are convinced that Black James, and not Sir Singleton, fired at Sir Lionel?"

Reginald faced him bravely.

"I am convinced," he said.

"And the other stories? the money which was stolen, and the debts—and do you still think that he was insane?"

"On those points I shall explain myself to Sir Singleton himself. Once more, good evening, Mr. Seldon."

"Lucifer was a baby in pride to you," muttered the incensed lawyer, as his visitor disappeared. "But one comfort remains: that beautiful Miss Trelawney escaped you."

CHAPTER XIII.

ARRIVED at home again, Reginald gave orders for the packing of his portmanteau, and for the safe keeping and kind treatment of the negro during his absence; and then, hearing that Marian was in the drawing-room, he went thither to speak to her. He found her waiting for him, in all the glories of pink silk and Honiton lace—and a bad temper. But this last was nothing uncommon. Mrs. Hamilton said of herself that she "absolutely *required* excitement." Which, in plain English, meant that she was very cross unless she was amused.

"Not dressed yet, Reginald?" she cried out when she saw him.

"Dressed!" he answered absently. "Was I going with you? Oh! I forgot all about it, Marian. I really beg your pardon—but I cannot go. I have—I had an adventure this evening. I have found Black James."

"And pray, who is Black James?"

"Why—Sir Lionel Trelawney's servant; you remember, don't you?"

"Oh yes, I know now. It was he whom Singleton accused of firing at his father. Has he confessed?"

"He has. It was he, and not Singleton."

Oh, foolish Marian! can you not hear the agony in his voice? Lay your hand upon his shoulder, and say tenderly, "God help you, my dear husband!" Give him a little sympathy in his sore need, and he will love you as he never did before: for he needs it, and will never forget that you gave it.

But Marian's answer was:

"Of course! I was always sure of it."

"You were sure of it! Why, Marian, you have told me a hundred times that you believed firmly in Singleton's guilt!"

"My dear, you were determined to believe it, and to believe him insane, and I don't know what else. I never set up for a heroine, so I seldom contradict you, it was no affair of mine. But what has all this to do with your coming, as you promised, to D—— House to-night?"

"I cannot go—" he began.

"There is nothing on earth to prevent it," she interrupted. "People are beginning to remark that we are seldom together, and I don't choose to be talked about. Go and dress—I will wait for you."

"I cannot, Marian. I could not bear it—and besides, I am going to Plymouth by the night train."

Mrs. Hamilton lost her temper on hearing this.

"Indeed!" said she with a pink spot coming in her cheeks. "To carry him the news, I suppose? You feel, no doubt, that it will be doubly welcome coming from an old and faithful friend and affectionate brother-in-law!"

"I feel," Reginald answered slowly, "that I have—wronged him, and that I want to say 'forgive me!'"

"Indeed!" she said again. "Very touching, very humble, very everything else that is not like you, Reginald. Are you sure that there is no one else at the Abbey whom you feel you have wronged? no one else whose forgiveness would be a comfort to you? Do you really think that I am such a fool as to believe that you go there to see Singleton Trelawney only?"

The words "You may believe what you like," rose to his lips, but he did not say them. Suppressing even a movement of impatience, he said gently:

"I think, Marian, that you have no reason to suspect me of falsehood: so when I say that I sincerely wish that I could see Singleton only, I expect to be believed."

"What gratifying intelligence that would be to your mother and father, whom you have not seen I don't know when—and your sister whom you have never seen since her marriage. Your uncle is there too, isn't he?" inquired Marian with assumed carelessness.

"I was not thinking of them when I spoke," replied Reginald with more truthfulness than discretion. She turned upon him in a moment.

"And of whom, then, were you thinking?"

He reddened, but made no answer.

"Ah!" she went on, "you cannot even attempt to deny it. For you, the only person at the Abbey is—Haidee Trelawney. Reginald, if you go there I will never forgive you."

"My dear Marian——"

"Don't call me your dear Marian! I know you never cared for me. You married me for my money—you know it is true. You *never* cared for me," she went on, working herself into a passion.

He had wonderful patience with her generally, but this night he was excited and less able to control himself than was his wont. He walked over and sat down beside her—she, in spite of her emotion, carefully drawing away her precious lace flounces from contact with his somewhat dusty boots.

"Now, Marian," he said, "as you are so much your own mistress that you can still care for your finery, be silent for a moment and listen to me."

Surprise kept her silent. She very seldom succeeded in making him angry, he did not care enough about her for that.

"I mean to go to Trelawney Abbey to-night: and I shall not be stopped by your folly:—for folly it is, as you know very well. You don't even believe it yourself. You don't really suspect that I have any other reason for going than the one I have given you. And now, one word more. This is not the first time that you have informed me that I married you for your money. Now, never let me hear you say it again. I have no wish to be unkind, but that is a thing no man could submit to:—and you have no right to say it."

"Why not, if it be true?"

"Because I never deceived you, for a moment. You knew exactly how it was with me, and you declared yourself content with such love as I had to give. And I don't think I have been a bad husband to you."

"O no," she answered, trembling with rage and spite (no other word could express it). "Not a bad husband at all, as times go. You have not beaten me—nor locked me up! O no —a model husband, though not of the gushing order. Go to the Abbey by all means: I was a fool to care about it. Give my best congratulations to Sir Singleton. I wonder if he is half as fond of that little white-faced Hester as he was once of me. And if you *should* happen to remark to Miss Trelawney that it is a pity the truth did not come out sooner, you may add that even now it might not have been too late if she had never written that impertinent letter to me. She will tell you that I am not a safe person to offend."

"What do you mean? Explain yourself, Marian."

"With pleasure. You have kindly reminded me that you did not deceive me by pretending to be in love with me—at least not very much in love; but did you fancy that I was very much in love with you? for if you did, either I am a very good actress, or you are very easily taken in."

"Why did you marry me, then?"

"I married you, my dear, because I knew that if the truth about Singleton ever came out, there would be a touching scene of reconciliation, and that then you would marry Haidee Trelawney. I hated her, and was determined to prevent that. I did not do it to spite you: I rather liked you, and thought that as *I* wanted to be married, and *you* wanted money—but I forgot: I'm not to say that. I did it for the sake of revenge on that high and mighty young lady, who once when Singleton was ill, sent me such an insolent answer to a note of inquiry I wrote to her. I vowed revenge,—and I have it."

She rose and rang the bell.

"Is the carriage at the door? You will have to get a cab to take you to the station, Reginald. Good-bye—I suppose I shall see you when you come back."

It may easily be imagined that Reginald's feelings, not very pleasant to begin with, were even less pleasant now. As he mechanically put her lace shawl and warm mantle over her shoulders, and watched her gathering up her gloves, fan and flowers, he felt rather as if he were dreaming. In looking back upon his marriage, he had always taken some comfort in thinking that at all events it had been for Marian's happiness, because she loved him: and behold, she had hated poor Haidee much more warmly than she had loved him.

Marian went off triumphant : she had at least silenced him and had the last word. Excitement had given her a colour, and she was much admired that evening at D—— House.

While she danced and flirted, and otherwise amused herself, her husband, all alone in the dimly-lighted railway carriage, sat thinking—writing bitter things against himself. He could not sleep, but in the quiet his mind recovered from the shock, and he could think.

And he thought of many things. Of his past life, once so full of happy promise: now so "flat, stale, and unprofitable." The comfort he had been wont to take in laying the blame on others, he had now lost : the fault, the blindness, the mistake, had been his, and his alone. He could not blind himself to that ; indeed he did not try to do so, but confessed it all, and with bitter, heart-wrung tears (tears of which he was utterly ashamed, though he had no need to be) he told himself the truth about himself, and found in himself a severe and uncompromising judge. If it be true that "Before honour is humility," Reginald Hamilton had never been so worthy of honour as he was during that wretched night, when he passed his life in review before his conscience, and told himself that it was a failure, and that by his own act.

It was a miserable night: and yet there was a more peaceful look upon his handsome face than there had been for many a day, when he left the railway carriage in the Plymouth station.

It was only seven o'clock. Too early to go on to the Abbey: and besides he was dusty and travel-stained, haggard and spent with hunger and sorrow. It was not altogether pride which made him unwilling to present himself before his—judges, as he almost called them—in this condition. He would ask forgiveness, but would not extort it by his wretched appearance.

Poor Singleton would never have thought of this, but would have rushed in, wild and breathless, and been called un-English, if not mad, for his pains.

Reginald went to the Royal Hotel, bathed and dressed and tried to breakfast: then ordered a cab and set forth along the well-known road, where at every turn a memory was waiting for him. O that ride home! that day when he and Haidee, graceful, loving, spirited Haidee, had lost themselves in the lanes. But he forced his thoughts away from that.

It was eleven o'clock when he reached the Abbey;—eight years now, since he had come there last and met Haidee and Singleton in the porch. Pierce knew him, and breathed hard, after the manner of servants when surprised.

"Is Sir Singleton at home?"

"Yes, sir. He is on the terrace with my lady;" and Mr. Pierce added the private reflection, "As 'aughty as ever," in consequence of Hamilton's failing to notice him. Whereas poor Reginald hardly saw him, and was maintaining a calm demeanour only by a violent effort.

"I will go to him. Can I pass this way?" he said, and walked past the servants into a small room in which there was a door leading to the terrace.

"You need not come with me," he said. "I shall announce myself."

Pierce looked unutterable things, but withdrew as desired. The unfortunate object of his wrath went out upon the terrace, and looked about for Singleton and Hester. They were there, as Pierce had said; but there were others there, whom Pierce had not mentioned. On a couch under the great cedar lay Captain Hamilton, and at the foot of the couch sat Haidee, with a newspaper in her hand which she appeared to be reading aloud. At her feet, upon the grass, appeared a heap, with a vision of little red shoes and white arms flourishing above it. This, as he drew near, Reginald perceived to be Singleton, prone on his back, with his son and heir lying on him, and kicking his small heels in the air with infinite satisfaction to both parties. Hester stood near; and she was the first to see her brother. And being, as we are aware, given to knowing things by intuition, she no sooner saw his face, than she knew pretty well what had happened.

She started forward with heightened colour; but even then she had a thought for others. She touched Haidee and whispered:

"Do you see, Haidee? look, it is he!"

Singleton heard, and raised his head; with a bound he was upon his feet, having rolled little Lionel over on to the grass, where he sat staring, his baby dignity much outraged.

Reginald came on—Singleton stood irresolute. He was cruelly embarrassed. The only time he had seen Hamilton for many years had been when they met on the steps of the house in Russell Square. He had been cold as ice then; what brought him here—how should he greet him now? Should he offer his hand? Would Reginald take it?

But before he could act, or Hamilton speak, Hester had caught her brother's hand, and gasped out breathlessly:

"You know the truth! Is Black James found?"

"Hester, what *are* you saying?" cried Singleton.

"I am right! I know I am right, Reginald."

"You are right, Hester." And then, putting her gently aside, he looked imploringly at his old friend; who, startled and puzzled, stared blankly at them both.

"Singleton! don't you know what has happened—don't you understand? Reginald says that Black James has been found."

Haidee, who had drawn near, laid her hands upon Reginald's arm and said in a low voice:

"And did *you* find him? Oh, Reginald, God help you!"

She covered her face with her hands, and fled into the house. She

> "——could not endure the face to see,
> Of the man she had loved so tenderly."

Singleton started as if from a dream.

"You've found old James?" he said.

"I have. I know the truth now, Singleton."

Captain Hamilton was sitting up on the couch

and looking at them; Mr. and Mrs. Hamilton, attracted by the sound of Haidee's sobbing, were coming from the porch to see what was going on; Singleton looked at his old friend, and the expression of shame and humility upon the calm, proud face, was more than the great generous heart could bear. No other eyes must see it.

"Come with me,—this way; and tell me how it happened."

"No, not alone, Singleton! I wronged you before all the world, and if possible, I would confess my error before all the world. Black James came to me last night, and Phillips has been with Seldon. Your innocence and John Trelawney's guilt are proved beyond the possibility of doubt."

Singleton bowed his head.

"Thank God," he said, in a tone of such heartfelt gratitude that the two words conveyed a whole volume of meaning. Then the two men looked at each other, and with one impulse the others left them alone; even the poor mother, whose heart was yearning over her son, went silently away; and Francis Hamilton, who could not move from his sofa, turned his back upon them, either to conceal his own emotion, or not to see theirs.

"Singleton! I am ashamed to look you in the face. I have wronged you beyond forgiveness. I have shown myself unworthy of trust or love. I never understood you, or did you justice. I hardly know how to ask you to forgive me. Yet —if you could see——"

He stopped abruptly; he could speak no more. Singleton looked at him, wistfully and sadly at first; then with a most uncertain smile flickering over his face, he put his two hands on Hamilton's shoulders, and said:

"Reginald, I suppose you would never be content unless I said it. I forgive you. You have suffered more than I have."

Then suddenly he clasped him, boyish fashion, round the neck, and sobbed aloud; then drawing back with a broken laugh, he said:

"Un-English! Regie. Very un-English still, I'm afraid."

But not more un-English at that moment than poor Hamilton himself, who broke down completely at the sound of the word.

"Oh, Trelawney! you may forgive, but I shall never forgive myself. Heaven help me! what a hard ungenerous beast I have been."

"Look here!" exclaimed Francis Hamilton, suddenly sitting up, and speaking in a very gruff voice. "Do you know that I'm here, you two? I can't run away, you know. Reginald, my dear boy, come here to me. I was feeling very hard to you—thinking that you had spoiled my—but no matter. No man can do more than say he knows his faults and is sorry! and you'll kill this soft-hearted lad if you go on like this. Look at him."

Reginald looked and saw that Singleton was nearly exhausted; though his face wore an expression of peace and serenity which was wonderful to see. Hester, who was watching them from the porch, now came out again, with the baby in her arms; Singleton took him from her.

"Look at this young gentleman, Reginald! He'll be a truer Trelawney than ever I was, don't you think?"

"Reginald, papa and mamma want you; and I will show you their room. I will not allow any more agitating talk until after luncheon, we know enough until then."

She led him away.

"You see, Regie, I have to be very careful of him; he is never very strong. So you won't think me unkind. This is the room. Regie, kiss me!"

He stooped and kissed her, and held her

hand in his, trying to speak. But words would not come, and he turned away silently.

What passed between that son and his parents, so long estranged, no one ever knew. But from that day all the old love and confidence was restored between them.

CHAPTER XIV.

A LETTER from Mr. Seldon to Singleton arrived by the mid-day post. Phillips had not appeared at the appointed time, and the lawyer did not like to leave town while there was any chance of his coming. He had seen Black James, who was ready to do anything he was desired, to clear his master's name: and the poor old man was so ill that Mr. Seldon had sent a doctor to see him, who thought very badly of his case. All his cry was to see Mr. Singie "just once more." Mr. Seldon then expressed his joy at the turn affairs had taken in terms of real affection, and then went on thus:

"When I think that this unlucky old negro was in London all this time, while I have been spending your money in searching for him everywhere else, I am ready to hang myself for my own stupidity. I did make inquiries here, too, but one has no chance in such a wilderness."

He then went into the question of legal proceedings against John, over which Singleton shook his head. He was reading the letter for the benefit of the whole party, as they sat under the cedar, enjoying their afternoon tea. Reginald was there, spent and pale as if after a severe illness: and Haidee was there, in a state of suppressed excitement which made her talkative, and raised her colour in a most becoming way.

"What are you shaking your head about, Singie? No, don't look at Hester, as much as to say 'she knows.' No doubt she does know; but I don't set up for a witch, and so I can't know till I am told."

"You are *not* going to let that rascal off?" exclaimed Captain Hamilton.

" Well—look here!" began Singleton just in his old way; " I have been thinking about it all day, and my mind is made up. I hope I shall convince you that I am right, but I am quite sure that I am, myself."

"You are always so modest, dear Sing. Go on."

"I did not mean that exactly, of course; what I mean to say is, that thinking as I do, I could not act otherwise."

"Otherwise than quite rightly! I see that, of course," remarked Haidee gravely.

"No, you torment. Otherwise than as I am going to tell you. You see, Seldon confesses that it would be both difficult and expensive to bring John to book for his misdoings: and I am not rich enough, thanks to him, to undertake a long and expensive law affair, merely for revenge, or a chance of it, rather. For it comes to that, you see. There is nothing else to be got by it. I have no hope of doing him any good. I have no hope of recovering the money he cheated my poor father out of. It is evidently doubtful that I could prove his guilt, legally, though I might make it morally clear enough. And then there is another side to the question."

"Now, Singleton," said Mr. Hamilton. "I hope it is not that you dislike the publicity, or anything of that sort. You ought not to give way to that feeling now. And I shall be very sorry, I may as well confess, if John Trelawney escapes. It has been all his doing—all this misery."

"Not *all* his doing, sir. The mischief was partly my own doing. If I had not been a headlong, thoughtless idiot, I should never have had any dealings with him, as Hester told me at the time; and then with all the will in the world he might never have been able to injure me. And if I had tried to behave as I ought to my father, instead of letting John have it all his own way, matters might have been very different."

"All the same, I never called you an idiot, Singleton," said Hester.

"You gave me good advice, my lady! and if I had asked for it before, instead of after the mischief was done, we should have had quieter lives."

"Yes," said Haidee hastily; "but now go on, Singleton, now that you have completely proved that you alone are to blame for John's wickedness and poor papa's blindness, and, in fact, that but for you we should all have been angels—tell us why you don't wish to punish John."

"Because, though John was the moving spirit of the scheme, my poor father was the instrument. I cannot expose John without letting Sir Lionel appear either as his accomplice or his dupe. Now, just because I was not a dutiful son, I ought to be more careful to—be dutiful now, when he can't defend himself."

"He found John out at the last," said Haidee.

"Yes—this copy of what Phillips told Seldon explains that. He overheard them talking.

And don't you remember telling me, Haidee, how my poor father's cry was for time to do justice? He never meant to be unjust; and it would be unjust now to set the whole world talking of his mistakes."

They all tried, Reginald in particular, to persuade him that this view of his duty was rather overstrained: but Singleton stood firm. He would do nothing to expose Sir Lionel to obloquy.

"Then what do you think of doing, Trelawney? for something, surely, you will do."

"Oh, yes. I shall run up to town to-morrow —see Seldon, and decide on the best way of making the matter public. For my own part, I don't care now so much about the public, but for the children's sake it must be done."

Hester looked over at him and nodded, with a smile, which he seemed to understand.

"Yes, you were right, Hester."

"And yet you never left off fretting about it: did you, now?"

"No—I could not," he answered, looking away over the wide landscape, with a dreamy gaze. "I did so dread seeing *that* look in their eyes."

"Now, did any one ever know such a provoking pair?" inquired Haidee of the company generally. "They look at each other and say a disconnected word or two; and *they* know all about it, and don't care whether any one else does or does not. Singleton, when shall you go to town?"

"When Hamilton goes. Regie, come with me, I want to show you the church. You have seen none of our improvements yet."

"You will stay with me—with us?" said Reginald, following him.

"Certainly, if you can have me."

They walked away arm-in-arm. The party left under the cedar were silent for some time. Francis Hamilton was watching Haidee very earnestly, as she followed with her eyes the two who had gone away. The three ladies were seated on the grass, Mrs. Hamilton in the midst; and Hester had some red roses in her hand, which she was idly arranging and re-arranging.

Presently Haidee said :

"Hester, how strangely a bit of the past comes back on one sometimes. Do you remember our sitting here, you and I and mamma, just as we are sitting now, and you were putting some of those very roses into the great tall glass thing, that Pierce broke last year."

"I remember it well! I was thinking of it too.

And how you consulted mamma about Singleton; and mamma sorely disconcerted me by watching me all the time, till I was so nervous that the roses toppled out as fast as I put them in."

"I remember it too," said Mrs. Hamilton. "For your face told me that I had lost my last child, Hester. I saw that you were a woman, and that you were beginning to find it out."

"But the scene had an ending which none of you knew of," said Hester. "Do you remember that we heard Sir Lionel's voice, and you told me to carry the roses in, that he might see that we were near?"

"No, I had forgotten that."

"I carried them in—and in the porch I met poor Black James, in a great fright: and Sir Lionel very angry. James had been caught listening, I think. Poor Sir Lionel! he was very kind to me."

"Because you were good to him. Hester, you are the only one among us, I mean of us four, who can look back and say 'No part of the misfortunes has been my fault.'"

Hester only shook her head in her old fashion. Mrs. Hamilton rose.

"Henry, my dear, come in now. It is time for you to rest a little."

"Come and read to me then: Hester, my dear old woman, I can't get over it at all. I am utterly disgusted that John Trelawney should escape."

"So am I!" said the sailor savagely. "Ah! if I could have him on board ship for an hour or so. I'd give him four dozen, well laid on. And yet I know that Singleton is right."

"Right! of course he is right!" said Hester, with a comfortable conviction which made them all laugh. "And pray what have I said to amuse you so much? You are very easily diverted, ladies and gentlemen. I am going to the nursery. Haidee, you can stay with Uncle Frank, can't you?"

Haidee got up from the grass and seated herself at the foot of the Captain's sofa.

"I have the *Times* here," she said. "You have not read it yet, so I had better begin."

"Never mind the *Times* yet a bit, Haidee," said the Captain, in whose mind her expression 'we four' was rankling sadly. "I have fifty things to say to you. Are you, like Hester, convinced that Singleton is right?"

"Well—yes. I am wicked you know, and Hester is good, so I am more vexed than she is that John should escape. But I know how people would talk of poor papa."

"The rascal injured you more than he did Hester," said the Captain in a low voice. Haidee made no reply.

"Poor Reginald," said Francis Hamilton reflectively. "He looks very unhappy."

Still there was no answer.

"Haidee."

"Well, Captain Hamilton?"

"Why don't you answer when I speak to you?"

"You did not ask me any question, you know, you only made a remark."

"But then I meant you to make another."

"How was I to know that? and I had none ready, besides."

"I wish—I wish I could see into your heart, Haidee."

"You would see nothing there that you—are thinking of," she answered quickly. "And if I don't read the *Times* now, we shan't have time for it before dinner."

She accordingly read: but I doubt if he heard much of it. "You would see nothing there that you are thinking of." What on earth *could* she mean? The reading was still going on when Reginald and Singleton returned.

"Now, my Captain! will you stay here while we are at dinner, or shall I call up a boat's crew and get you comfortably back into your room?"

"I'll go to my room, I think. I'm tired, Singleton—the day is so hot."

Singleton called two of the servants, and they wheeled off the sofa gently. Haidee was watching the removal rather anxiously, and not until her patient was out of sight did she seem to remember Hamilton. Then she turned to make some trivial remark, but the look she met silenced her. Such a glance of mute agony— of a desire to speak, and a fear of offending her. She said nothing for a moment, and then looked again at him. Their eyes met. Haidee knew so well what he was longing to say, and dared not: and after another moment's hesitation her generous impulse to give him what comfort she could, overcame her embarrassment. She drew a little nearer to him and said :

"Reginald, do not look at me as if you thought I had bitter feelings towards you. It is not so, indeed. Once, I was very bitter against you, but now I can say with perfect truth that I have long ceased to think of the past—so far as it concerned me—with regret. I am very happy, Reginald; and you are my brother's friend—and mine," she added, holding out her hand to him.

He was an honest man, and for one moment

he felt as if he must say, "I dare not touch your hand—I cannot be your friend," but he controlled himself.

"Thank you," he said. "It is more to me than you could believe to hear those words. God bless you, Haidee. It is right that things should be as they are—I was utterly unworthy of you."

"Don't say that, I was to blame too. Let us forget the past now, from this moment."

"Be it so," he answered, with a strange smile. "I am glad you have forgiven me, Haidee; and I hope you may have a bright and happy future. He is—all that I was not."

Haidee blushed crimson, and left him, looking back from the porch with a smile, to show that she was not angry. Singleton came out again in a minute.

"Reginald! I have kept you running about in the sun till you look like a ghost."

"Do I look like one who has had 'coals of fire heaped upon him'? for that is what you and yours have been doing. But, Singleton, it shall prove a purifying fire—not a consuming one. Old friend—I cannot put it into words, but believe me I feel deeply the way in which I have been received by you all."

In his own room, while dressing for dinner,

Reginald's mind dwelt upon Haidee's words, and the noble air of simple, frank dignity with which she had spoken.

"There is not," he thought, "another woman in the world who would have answered my look as she did. And yet there was a time when I was idiot enough to quarrel with her frankness. Well! I have learned to value it now."

Next day, Reginald returned to London, and Singleton went with him.

CHAPTER XV.

In about a week, Singleton Trelawney returned from London : to find his family in a great state of indignation with him, inasmuch as he had written to them but seldom, and what was worse had given them hardly any news in his letters, except the somewhat startling intelligence that Black James was dead.

"But I was kept so busy, you have no idea. I assure you I found it impossible to write long letters. And besides, when I was coming home in a week, where was the use of writing? it's much pleasanter to tell it all."

"Tell it all then! that's the only amends you can make. Tell us all and everything, and perhaps we may forgive you."

"I'm sure I am quite willing, Haidee. First, as you know, I saw Seldon; and after a sharp engagement he hauled down his colours, and confessed that I was right. Phillips had never come back — did I tell you that?"

"You told us nothing!" said Haidee.

"He had found out that Black James had told all, I suppose," remarked Hester.

"No doubt. Poor old James. He made a regular sworn confession before a magistrate : I was with him night and day until he died. Poor affectionate, foolish old fellow! his sorrow would have touched a stone."

"I was almost glad to hear of his death," Haidee said. "What was to become of him?"

"Indeed it was as well. I don't think myself that he was quite accountable for his actions— but he repented, and no man can do more."

"But what vexes me," said Mr. Hamilton, "is, that the negro's confession does not clear up the matter about the asylum. I do wish that could be set right : for your children's sake."

"Well, sir, no sooner had I got my own way, and made every one agree to leave it alone, than I began to feel as you do. So after much cogitation, I made up my mind to try—an experiment. To that end I bought a revolver."

"My dear Singleton! what for?"

"Self defence, Lady Trelawney. And as things turned out, I never wanted it; but had I gone without it, you would have been the very first to accuse me of rashness, folly, and an unnatural desire to make you a widow."

"If you had gone! where *have* you been? Oh Singleton, what dreadfully imprudent thing have you been doing?"

"And this is what the feebler sex call consistency! As I was provided with a pistol, I was in no danger. I went and saw—who, do you think?"

"John!" cried Haidee. "Ah—I knew it; and you made him tell the truth, I hope."

"A new sensation for him, if he did," said Francis Hamilton.

"Before I went," Singleton proceeded, "I wrote down the heads of what I wanted him to say, for fear I should make a mess of it. Then I went to his house. He had no idea I would go myself, though he said he was expecting to hear from me."

"Why did he stay there, then?"

"If I may believe him, because Phillips had tyrannized over him, and plundered him to such an extent, that he was determined to dare the worst rather than be still under his thumb. Anyhow there I found him, sitting all alone with a lot of bottles and glasses all about."

"And how did he look?"

"Haidee, I declare I think one might pass

him by in the street and not know him. Like my father! not a bit of it. He's as fat as a pig, with a great red bottle nose and bloodshot eyes. Haidee, used he to drink in the old days? he does now, certainly."

"I used to suspect him sometimes."

"Well—I reasoned the matter with him quietly: and I must say he was civiller than I expected, and the task was rather easy on the whole. I told him that he certainly got Sir Lionel to leave him all that money, which was my mother's money to make it even worse, by making him believe a whole pack of lies, and that I should have a decent case against him if I chose to try it. But that for Sir Lionel's sake I wished to avoid that; and that if he would confess to two things, he might keep the money."

"And he—what did he say?"

"That Phillips had had more than half the money—but after some bother and shilly-shally talk, he consented."

"What were the two things? the debts—and——"

"No, no, sir! not the debts. That did not really matter now. No: I made him say that he met me as I stated, the evening Sir Lionel was shot: and that he had procured my being sent to a lunatic asylum, knowing me to be sane."

"And you made him write this himself? By Jove! Singleton, I would give a hundred pounds to have been by. Ancient Pistol eating his leek was a joke to it."

"Here it is, my Captain; in his own very tipsyfied claw. Then I said: 'John, I don't suppose that even you are so hardened as not to care for the contempt which this will bring upon you—so I give you two days to get out of England, and I advise you never to return.' Then I made him my best bow, and marched off triumphant, to rejoice Reginald's heart—for he was quite unhappy that my sanity was not to be proved."

"And what were you to do in the two days, Singleton?"

"Publish that paper and poor James's confession in the *Times, Daily News, Army and Navy*, etc., etc. It's in the daily papers to-day —where's the *Times?* look—here it is—and there's a notice of it in another part, which Reginald wrote."

"Well, Singleton! I am thoroughly glad you have done this," Mr. Hamilton said. "For I may tell you now, that I had a little idea that you spared John as much for my poor boy's sake as for your father's : and if that had struck him, it would have made him miserable."

"I was bound to think of Sir Lionel," was all the answer Singleton made. "John told me he thought of going to America."

"I don't care where he goes," said Haidee. "And I don't know how *you* contrived to talk to him about his conduct, without pouncing upon him and shaking the nasty mean soul out of him."

"He is at least double my size, my energetic friend; and no doubt that exercised a composing influence on me. And besides, he was wonderfully civil."

"Which would have only made me more angry. Where was Phillips, by the way?"

"Oh, gone, of course. Got a last few pounds out of John and made off. So there, as far as we are concerned, is an end of John Trelawney and his trusty Jaspar."

"Any more news, Singleton?"

"Well—I dined with, or in company with, all the upper ten, I think. And wished myself quietly at home all the time. I don't know which is the pleasanter, to be stared at as a sinner and possible maniac, or as a curiosity which every one had quite forgotten, until it was dug up all of a sudden. Every one was very kind, though—and I saw the first lord, and he offered me an appointment, if I wished to go to sea."

"And you said: 'No, sir! I have a wife and two children, and so *you* may get on as best you can without me, for *they* can't.'"

"I did. And he howled with anguish, and said the supremacy of the British navy was now a thing of the past."

"Singleton, tell me about my dear Regie," said Mrs. Hamilton; "and Marian—was she pleasant to you?"

This was a little later, and the speaker was alone with her son-in-law.

"O yes, quite pleasant."

"How does she look?"

"Much the same: a little pale of a morning, but bright and pretty of an evening."

"And the children? what are they like? I fancied poor Reginald rather disliked being asked about them."

Singleton made an expressive face.

"They are rather pretty," he said. "But indeed I did not see much of them. They are not—what you would call taking children. They are so pleased with themselves and like little women you know. And they seemed to cry a good deal: I used to hear them often."

"And Singleton—tell me plainly—how do Reginald and Marian get on?"

"He is kind, and gentle, and considerate—forbearing to the last degree. But the misfortune is, he can't help seeing when she is manœuvring, or saying what is not quite the case; and she is angry at being always found out. He would be happier if he were blinder."

"I knew it would be so. Poor Arthur never saw it."

"No—nor did I, in the old times at Halifax. It is only in looking back that I see it."

"You would not have remained blind, though."

"Reginald is very busy, you know. I went to the House to hear him speak one night, and felt so proud of him: he speaks so clearly and concisely and his voice is so good. Regie will be a great man yet, Mrs. Hamilton."

"I would rather see him a happy one. Ah, my poor Regie," murmured his mother, half unconsciously.

Great was the excitement at Trelawney Abbey and in the neighbourhood for the next few days. Tar barrels and bonfires blazed on every height, and the farmers came in a body to the Abbey to wish Sir Singleton joy. It was surprising how many people now declared that they had never believed a word against him.

Then "the neighbourhood" called: and so did the naval society of Plymouth, a tolerable sprinkling of the military society also. Pierce and his satellites were worn out with opening doors and announcing guests: and Haidee was very tired of the guests. But Hester took every visit as a fresh tribute to Singleton's merits, and received them all with a gentle flutter of triumph that was very pretty. How often she told the story of the finding of Black James, who can tell? but she at least was never tired of it, and was quite ready to tell it again.

"So then," said Singleton Trelawney, in telling his adventures to his wife and sister, "there is an end of John and his trusty Jaspar, as far as we are concerned." But he was very much mistaken.

Perhaps some people may like to know what became of John Trelawney, and although the family at the Abbey heard nothing of him for some years, I had better conclude his history here. He went to America, and there fell in with Phillips again. Together they established themselves as merchants in New Orleans, and made a good deal of money for some years.

But being forced to fly from the city in consequence of some nefarious dealings, of which John declared that Phillips alone was guilty, while Phillips imputed all the blame to John, they lost everything they possessed. Phillips was never heard of again, but John came home to England: and now drags on a wretched existence, supported by a small pension from his cousin, Sir Singleton, of whom he brags to his low companions when half drunk, and whom he accuses of having ruined him when quite drunk. And half drunk or quite drunk (he can hardly ever be said to be sober) he is just the same John Trelawney still—and, it is to be feared, will be so to the end.

CHAPTER XVI.

UNDER the cedar-tree once more.

Captain Hamilton (now able to sit up in an easy-chair), Hester and Singleton deep in conversation.

"So you see," says the Captain, "I give it up."

"And you show how little you know of women, Uncle Frank—and of Haidee in particular, though you *have* known her so long."

"And loved her so long," the sailor said with a sigh. "But I could not ask her to tie herself to a useless old cripple, which it seems I am to be for the future. No: I give it up."

Singleton said nothing, but with a nod to his wife, answered by a look from her brown eyes, he quietly walked away. He went into the house, and up to Haidee's room, where she sat in a wilderness of pink and green checked prints, cutting out frocks for the school-children.

"Is not this bad news, Haidee?" said he throwing himself down upon the sofa.

"What news? I have heard none."

"Well—the doctors have been with Captain Hamilton" (Haidee turned pale) "and have told him the truth—in fact he insisted on it. And it seems that the fracture of that little beast of a bone in the hip can never be cured. He'll be helpless always. It's a great pity."

"We—you—will take care of him," said Haidee, letting her scissors fall with a clatter.

"Shan't be allowed. He's going to live in London; with Mrs. Seymour."

"Why should he go? He never liked London and it won't agree with him at all. Why can he not stay here?"

"Well, I said that. I did all I could: but it's the old story, Haidee. Poor dear old Captain. You see he never cared for any one but you; and yet I know that you are right—it would never do."

"*What* would never do?"

"*That.* You couldn't marry him, you know. He might be your grandfather."

"Indeed he might *not*, Singleton. He is years younger than poor papa. It—it was not *that.*"

"Wasn't it? ah, but then you've known him

so long. You must think of him as a kind of guardian—or uncle; I see."

"No, indeed, you do *not* see, Singleton. I think of him as the best, kindest, truest friend—and the most delightful companion, I ever knew. It was not *that*."

"Well—at all events, you could not—you, young and strong and beautiful, tie yourself to a poor useless cripple, as he says himself. That would never do. But I'm very sorry for him. I owe him more than I can ever pay, and now when he really wants care, he'll go away and be miserable. I wish he had never thought of you in that way, Haidee;—it was very foolish of him."

"No, it was not! It was just like him—generous—noble—giving all and asking for nothing in return. If *you* owe him much, what do *I* owe him? What was I when he came here first? did I not learn first from his kind face that it was wrong to tell a lie? did he not get papa to send me to school, and persuade mamma to take me to her heart as if I were one of her own? And later—when my heart was nearly broken and my woman's pride bitterly mortified, did not he devote himself to me, without one thought of himself? And if in his long watching over me and caring for me, he has come to love me—oh Singleton! how can you go and call him a fool?"

"My dear, I did not go so far as that. I have too much respect for my superior officers."

To which I am sorry to state Haidee replied, "Oh bother your superior officer!"

"You have done that, my love."

"Singie—did he say all this to you lately?"

"All what?"

"That he must go away because—of me?"

"This morning, only a few minutes ago. I thought you ought to know. Pretty colour, that stuff."

Haidee made no answer, but applied herself to her cutting-out with so much more vigour than discretion, that she then and there spoiled and ruined six frocks out of her three dozen. Singleton watched her for a moment, smiled to himself, and returned to the old cedar.

"Hester, come along. I want you. I have something to consult you about."

Captain Hamilton was left alone. But he was not long alone. For in a moment a shadow came between him and the sun, and looking up he saw Haidee; with such an April beauty on her sweet face that she might have been seventeen once more. She looked at him for some time, her eyes begging him to speak; but the poor Captain was too unhappy to understand her eyes. So she knelt down beside him and said softly :

"You will not leave us!"

"I must, child. I know I am an old fool, and I cannot stay. Never mind, Haidee, you could not help it."

"You shall not go," she said slowly. He caught her hand.

"Oh, Haidee, I can stay only—oh, dear child, don't play with me. If you bid me stay, I shall stay—but do you know what that must mean?"

"I am not playing with you. Instead of telling Singleton, why did you speak to me?"

"Because since Reginald was here I have seen, or thought, that you would never listen to me or to any one else, in that way."

"To no one else, certainly."

"And to me, only because you pity me. Haidee, you'll think me very ungrateful—but that won't satisfy me."

"I don't pity you," she flashed out, springing to her feet. "You will be lame—but what of that? You have done work enough and may rest now. You will go to sea no more! that is one comfort."

"You don't pity me," repeated Francis Hamilton, staring at her.

"No, I should not think it—right; you are not made to be pitied. But I do think you very stupid—I do indeed."

"Haidee! Tell me, have I been mistaken? If you don't pity me, do you—love me?"

"Oh, Francis! I think I have loved you this long time, only I did not know it. It was not like what I felt long ago, and I thought I could never love again. But when he came I found myself perpetually comparing you with him, and thinking how much more gentle and good you have always been, and then I knew how it was with me."

After this confession, every right-minded person will be shocked to hear that when Singleton and Hester came back and heard the great news, Haidee gave a variety of reasons for consenting to be Francis Hamilton's wife; and not one of them was the true one,—that she loved him. She declared that it was because he could not walk without help, and her height suited him when he wanted an arm.

"But my dear, the real reason is, that it will produce such a delightful confusion in our relationships; and I have an ill-regulated mind and like the idea. I shall be your aunt, Singleton; and the children's grand-aunt, also your sister and their aunt. I shall be mamma's sister—I don't know how I should like to be addressed by little Lionel, 'Aunty grand-aunty.'—And Singleton, you must call me Aunt Haidee, mind. Altogether, if any one ever realized Mrs. Malaprop's ideas of Cerberus, by being three gentlemen at once, I shall be that person."

To which Singleton replied by asserting that *he* knew why she had consented at last—simply because he said she could not possibly do so.

But however the marriage was brought about, it has proved a very happy one.

And so the gale has passed away from the life of Singleton Trelawney, never, I hope to rage again. And thus I leave him, with more sorrow in the parting than I dare to hope any one else will feel. He has been my companion through many a stormy day in my own life, and I have grown quite fond of him; but my story is told, and so, farewell.

> "The book is completed
> And closed—like the day;
> And the hand that has written it
> Lays it away."

THE END.

BILLING AND SONS, PRINTERS, GUILDFORD, SURREY.

www.ingramcontent.com/pod-product-compliance
Lightning Source LLC
Chambersburg PA
CBHW032222230426
43666CB00033B/587